Best Wishes!

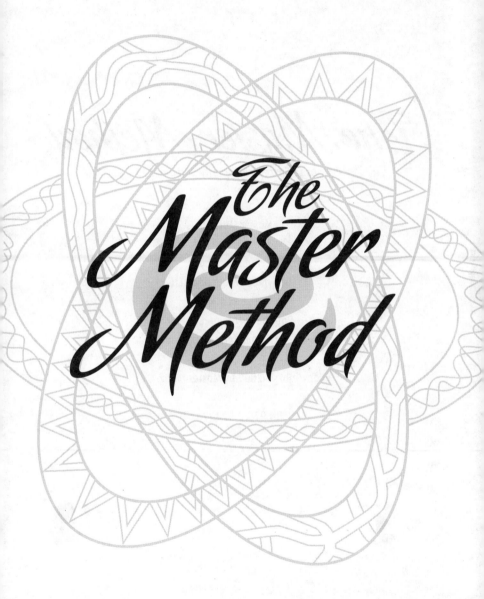

The Master Method

The Master Method

4 Steps to Success, Prosperity and Inner Peace

By
Master Marco Sies

Published by
Babyface Productions, LLC
P.O. Box 60433
Potomac, Maryland 20859
www.*themastermethod*.com

ISBN 978-0-9842262-0-7

Cover Icon Art: Jacqui Crocetta
Cover & Book Design: Connie Hameedi
Cover Photo: iStock.com
Back Cover Photo: Goli Kaviani
Editing: Richy Sharshan

In loving memory of my grandfather, Hector Vera,
who taught me what it truly means to be a gentleman.
His positive influence, joyful spirit and peaceful
soul are with me always.

Acknowledgements

I began writing *The Master Method* about two years ago and, although it's been a long journey, I've enjoyed every single step of the way. The process has taught me so much, and it has truly been a wonderful and exciting experience.

I would first like to acknowledge all of the great masters and teachers who came before us and left such valuable knowledge through their teachings and books. I was greatly influenced and learned what I know today not only from my experiences, but through the countless hours of reading and listening to the teachings of ancient and contemporary masters.

This book could not have been possible without Julie, who is soon to be my wife. To her, with all my love, I'm grateful, not just for this book, but for the opportunity to share each day with her and make this such a wonderful life. I am thankful for her love and constant support, combined with her guidance and her wonderful ability to transform my words and ideas into an organized and tangible manuscript. My gratitude is also with all our children, who give us so many reasons to be thankful and who allow us the opportunity to experience a life of pure happiness and joy. I look forward to spending each day with them and experiencing the highest level of unconditional love.

Thank you also to my friends and family who are so supportive and show such love. I feel blessed to have you all in my life.

This book is based on the concepts I teach, but it wouldn't have been possible without an absolutely amazing production team: Julie, working long hours every day, made sure everything moved along smoothly. Richy Sharshan, my editor, turned this book into an incredible work of art. She presented my story, preserving my words and concepts, but somehow crafted them into a masterpiece. David Baumann, who is not only my good friend and student, but also my wonderful web designer, developed an amazing website and provided us with his genius expertise. Jackie Crocetta, my friend of many years, so creatively took the essence of *The Master Method* and created the symbolic artwork for the book cover and icons within the book. Connie Hameedi, my book designer, who with her enormous amount of experience and knowledge, came and "saved the day" by so wonderfully putting everything together in the end. And Goli Kaviani, with her great artistic creativity, did a wonderful job on my cover portrait and other photographic needs. To all my team members, thank you! I'm forever grateful. They went above and beyond in all of their hard work and effort. I couldn't have asked for a better group of individuals to work with.

Most importantly, I would like to thank all of you for inspiring me to share this book with you. It is a true honor, and I humbly thank you for the opportunity to be your teacher.

With deepest gratitude,
Master Marco Sies

Contents

Introduction

Ancient Ideas for Modern Times

The teachings in this book, I could never credit to my own invention. Most of these ideas are ancient concepts that have been taught for thousands of years. The most influential people throughout history knew how to apply these theories and, if you look closely at their legacies, you will no doubt recognize many of the concepts presented in *The Master Method*.

Sharing My Knowledge and Life Lessons

I've spent my life studying the ancient masters and philosophers, as well as contemporary motivators and performance coaches. I gradually began to realize that, through these studies and my own life experiences, I had repeatedly used a particular successful process to help me reach my goals and to help my students, colleagues and family members reach theirs, whether it was an athletic endeavor, a business objective or other challenge. I created *The Master Method* to help others realize they control their own successes and their own happiness.

Compiling Universal Principles

In *The Master Method*, you'll find compiled, organized and applied to today's living, the wisdom of Jesus, Buddha, Mohammed, Hermes Trismegistus, Lao Tzu, Socrates, Plato and other teachers in ancient history. In addition, the most remarkable teachers of modern history and present times — His Holiness the Dalai Lama, Albert Einstein, Napoleon Hill, Mahatma Gandhi, Mother Theresa, Jack Canfield, Tony Robbins, Ester Hicks, Stephen Covey, etc. — have incorporated these same universal principles to help millions of people live better and realize success.

Success Comes with Practice

The Master Method is not a presentation of new concepts, but a new presentation of ancient and modern concepts. This book guides you in an easy, efficient and effective manner through these fundamental concepts and allows you to actively begin applying these concepts to your daily life immediately. Through my process, you can accomplish anything you desire, knowing you have the keys to open the beautiful gates of happiness, joy, abundance, wealth, prosperity and success in all areas of your life — finances, career, health, relationships and inner peace. By learning and implementing the simple four-step DCPC Formula (Desire, Condition, Plan, and Create!) you can start creating your ideal life RIGHT NOW.

~ Master Marco Sies

The Making of a Champion

It was a brutal left hook I will never forget that knocked me to the mat early in the second round of my first big fight in America. I knew at that moment I was completely outclassed. Stunned, I got back up, thinking to myself, "Even if I don't win this match, I will at least make this guy remember my name." I fought back fiercely and bravely, getting back up again and again until the referee ordered me to stay down late in the third round. And so ended the big debut of Marco "Babyface" Sies on national television.

You might have expected me to begin this book with one of my triumphant world championship victories ... or perhaps a poignant moment on the day I was inducted into the Karate World Hall of Fame as a Legend in Kickboxing. But I chose what some people would consider to be a disastrous failure for a good reason: to show that losing is nothing more than a big part of winning and, if you accept it as part of the process of achieving your goals, you'll become stronger and better equipped to continue toward your aspirations.

I ended up in the hospital that night, but with a conviction stronger than ever to become the fastest, smartest and technically best fighter on the planet. I later learned I had been set up against an Olympic champion by managers who assured me I would do fine, even though I was a kickboxer who had never trained in traditional boxing. Despite losing that fight, the heart I showed in those three rounds sparked a lot of interest in the baby-faced kid from South America, opening doors that led me closer to my dream. How did I develop the drive and determination that kept me on the path to success? It's a journey that began in the busy city of Santiago, Chile, where I was born.

A Small Boy. A Big Thinker.

I grew up in humble surroundings in Santiago, a city that's gritty and tough, but enchanting in its natural beauty, set in a lush valley at the foot of the Andes Mountains. Although my family's means were meager and I faced perhaps more than my share of troubles, I look back in appreciation to the people and experiences that shaped who I became and steered me toward my life today.

I was the oldest of three sons born to a mother and father who worked very hard to provide my brothers and me with the necessities and education every parent

wishes for his or her child. However, as kids, we didn't feel the struggle they must have experienced raising us, as we were just three little boys who found joy in the simplest of things. We spent hours outdoors getting as dirty as possible. We made several (thankfully unsuccessful) attempts at testing our parachuting abilities off the roof of our house. Always fascinated by nature, I remember hiding from, stalking, and eventually catching a variety of bugs, lizards, birds and other wild creatures with my bare little hands.

From an early age, I loved to read about the world around me, and I spent hours observing people, attempting to figure out why they behaved the way they did. At the age of eight, I read Carl Sagan's *Cosmos* and it intrigued me; were there humans on other planets? What was the cycle of life? Why are people the way they are? Why does the mind work as it does? An analytical child, I was fascinated with human psychology, fervently observing my parents, relatives and other adults, sometimes to their annoyance.

My warmest memories are of the wonderful times I spent fishing with my grandfather in the beauty and quiet of the trickling streams and pristine lakes high in the rugged mountains of Chile. My grandfather, whom we lovingly referred to as "Tata," not only taught me to fish, but he taught me how to live a life of true happiness and peace. To this day, I love to fish and I find great joy and tranquility in these moments.

My Tata was the kindest, gentlest and most humble soul I have ever known. He represented integrity, selflessness and honor — a true gentleman. He was my ultimate role model and the type of person I would spend my life striving to become. Despite some stumbling blocks of mistakes and bad choices I made along my journey, my Tata was always my grounding spirit and my foundation. He stood like a lighthouse guiding me to a wonderful place of peace, success, joy and fulfillment, and I am so grateful every day for this man's powerfully positive influence in my life.

Personal Struggles

Those fond recollections of childhood are the memories I choose to remember and on which I place my focus. However, growing up I also experienced difficulties and personal conflict that I've worked very hard to overcome. Some of these struggles stemmed from negative influences and people who told me I wasn't good enough ... I was inferior ... I wasn't smart ... I was too poor, too small, too unattractive to make anything of myself. I was told so many negative things so often, I actually spent many years believing these things were true.

Very small for my age, I was a dark-skinned boy living in a not-yet diversified population where light skin was admired and favored. At school, little girls told me I was ugly, and the boys bullied me relentlessly. I have stories, as so many children do, of schoolyard

taunting — I remember being thrown headfirst into a trashcan and also the humiliation of a group of boys whipping me with their neckties and making me run like a horse while they laughed. Even some of my own relatives made hurtful comments, all fueling my fears that I was unworthy and affecting my self-image, my confidence and my entire being. Added to that was a troubled relationship between my mother and father — a police detective and former military man with traditional macho ideas.

Looking back on those years, knowing what I know now, I see how some of these negative childhood experiences stayed with me well into adulthood and heavily influenced the way I handled relationships, among other things. I now understand that these experiences were necessary to help me identify what I *didn't* want for myself, realize how far I've come and better appreciate the life I have now.

Growing Up in a Macho World

As all boys do, I admired my father and uncles who were into the martial arts. By the age of five or six, I already had a fascination with kickboxing, persistently pleading with my dad to show me moves and "train" me. Although I wanted to be a great fighter, no one took this undersized boy seriously, and especially one who had his head buried in philosophy books most of the time.

People told me I was weird and crazy, but I had so many questions about the world around me and I finally felt validated when I discovered the writings of the great philosophers. And so I read Darwin and consumed everything I could find on Greek philosophy. Although I attended Catholic school, I studied the teachings of various religions — Muslim, Buddhist and even gnostic beliefs. Between the ages of 13 and 16, I wrote more than 100 essays on philosophy and psychology. Constantly studying the way people moved and behaved, I noticed, for example, the difference in the way my father interacted with his friends versus his family.

The negativity of my early childhood years started to change dramatically when I began to seriously study philosophy and meditation as a teenager. I signed up for a philosophy program at one of our local schools, not realizing it was subsidized by donations and student support. I was the only youngster in a class of adults. When it came time to make a contribution, a kindhearted woman in my class made a donation on my behalf when she saw I had nothing to give. Because of her generosity, I was able to continue my studies. I also continued my martial arts training, determined to prove the doubters wrong. At times, the subconscious thoughts and feelings from my childhood crept back, but now I had the principles I learned from ancient teachings to help me think positively and get back on track.

Life Changes and a New Determination

When I was 15, an exhibition by world champion kickboxer Bill "Superfoot" Wallace in my hometown changed the course of my life. I was awed by his power, mastery and discipline, and I decided that very night I wanted to become a world champion. I decided I WOULD become a world champion. I would train and learn and work harder than anyone ever had and let nothing stop me from reaching my goal. Of course when I shared my thoughts with others, they scoffed and laughed at me, but once my decision was made, I began to make my plan.

In summer of that same year, our father left and suddenly my mother was divorced and struggling to feed, clothe and educate three children. She had to work long hours to provide for our basic needs, so she was not in any position to help me with "luxuries" such as training to become the world champion! Some might have put their dreams aside, but I knew I had to make this work on my own.

I began working every job I could find to earn even the smallest amount of money, knowing every little bit would help. I washed dishes, I helped people carry groceries to their cars, I swept floors, and I even walked the several miles to and from school so I could save my bus money for training tuition. I was determined to accomplish my goal, and I knew this was going to help me get closer to it.

It was difficult at times, especially when I faced trying circumstances or negative influences from others whose "advice" or discouragement could have potentially diminished my faith. However, I somehow managed to keep my mind strong and maintain my focus on what I WANTED, rather than focusing on obstacles or the negative influences of others.

Believing and Staying the Course

Small opportunities began to fall into my path, and eventually, I was able to find work at a martial arts school cleaning floors, bathrooms and mirrors. I never looked at these duties as beneath me, but rather as an opportunity. Because I set out to become the *best* floor/bathroom/mirror cleaner, I soon earned more responsibilities and eventually the chance to begin assisting with martial arts classes. I realized that by doing *everything* with the best effort and enthusiasm, it would open the doors to increasingly better opportunities. AND it made me feel good in the process!

This first martial arts job allowed me to train and improve my martial arts and kickboxing skills, and after a couple of years of relentless, grueling work, I proudly became the Chilean National Champion. I was only eighteen years old, and it was an enormous achievement. I maintained my title for the next three years, but my eyes were still on the world title. Unfortunately, my odds of winning such a title were improbable if I remained in Chile. By age 21, I had accomplished all I could in South America and I knew I had to go to Europe or the United States, where there were more events, more promoters and more prospects for reaching my ultimate goal.

Coming to America

Expressing gratitude is an important part of my process of achieving success, and my journey to the U.S. began with two acts of kindness for which I will be forever grateful. The day before I left Chile, my beloved Tata came to say good-bye. To this day, I feel moved to tears remembering the gift he gave me that day with such great love and devotion —$40. Although a small amount to most Americans, it was his life's savings, put aside penny by penny. It was his way of showing he loved and supported me.

I will never forget his generous present, which was not about the money, but was a priceless gift of compassion and faith I cherish forever in my heart, knowing he believed in me. The other person who helped to make my quest possible was my Aunt Elizabeth, who lived in Virginia and allowed me to stay with her my first year in the States. In addition, she later gave me a job with her cleaning company.

And so I arrived in America with the $40 from Tata, a couple pair of pants and shirts, some music tapes and my martial arts uniforms. I was twenty-one years old and spoke very little English, but I was here to fulfill my dream of becoming the lightweight kickboxing champion of the world.

A New Nickname

I settled into an ambitious routine, working as a cleaner late at night, delivering newspapers in the early morning hours and still training at every opportunity. I also began to look for a promoter to represent me, but my baby face was proving to be a hindrance. No one believed I was old enough to fight! Things definitely seemed hopeless at times, and the challenges were many.

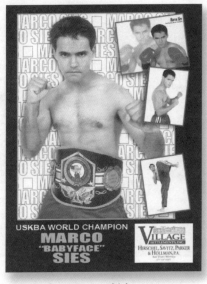

USKBA WORLD CHAMPION
MARCO
"BABYFACE"
SIES

I was a naive kid whose skills in a new language weren't the strongest. The world of kickboxing is a tough business with purses going mostly to the promoters and the actual fighter taking the physical punishment for only $200 or $300 per fight at most. We would often drive all night to get to an event and go straight to the weigh-in. I would fight and we would drive straight back home because hotel accommodations weren't in the budget. While the pay was far from enough to cover any bills, I knew I was building my reputation and my name, which now included a new nickname — I was now billed as Marco *Babyface* Sies.

In those early years, I met people who promised me training, fights and other "deals," but I didn't understand anything about contracts and was so green I assumed no one would be unethical or have bad intentions. At one point, I was convinced to travel to California with the promise of big money for just a couple of fights. I spent two months there and never got paid a dime. I returned to the East with nothing — no job, no money and no place to live.

Losing Everything

At this low point, I found myself homeless, and I didn't know where my next meal would come from. Despite these major setbacks, I never lost faith. I was so focused on becoming a world champion, things began to turn around. Without knowing why, I was accepting everything I experienced as part of my journey. Somehow I

knew I was being led closer and closer to my destination through these tests. Now, I look back on these hardships with gratitude for the lessons I learned. In hindsight, I realize each trial gave me the knowledge and tools I needed to become a kickboxing world champion. Even during the worst of times, I always believed I was on the path to becoming a world champion. I spent time meditating each day and my focus in those mediations was not on my current situation, but on my dream of where I wanted to be.

Within a few months I was back on my feet, and even though I had to work even harder to sustain myself, I didn't worry. I knew it was all part of the process. I couldn't afford a boxing gym, but I found an old couch near a dumpster, took the cushions off, tied them to a tree, and that became my punching bag! I trained in the parking garage at a local mall, running up and down the stairs, and I ran sprints in a local park. I used all the creative means I could think of to continue my training every single day in hot sun, rain or snow.

A Winner Emerges

Despite my first disastrous televised fight, another big fight eventually came my way. I actually knocked out the hometown favorite in an impressive victory in Rochester, New York. It was my first title in North America and I was joyously happy! The next day, I was told the president of the International Kickboxing Council, Grandmaster Keith Nesbitt, Sr., wanted to speak to me. He was impressed by my performance the night before and he was curious to know how I trained. He was shocked to hear I had no

training facilities and was deeply moved by my story. I returned home to find his associates had delivered all kinds of equipment so I could train properly. To this day, I am so thankful for the wonderful gesture from this kind Grandmaster who will always hold my deepest respect and admiration.

Beyond My Boyhood Dreams

After that victory, many fights came, as well as a great team of trainers and supporters. And in 2000, after twelve years of conditioning my mind and body, I was named the USKBA Super Lightweight Professional Full-Contact Kickboxing World Champion! The joy, excitement, pride and gratitude that washed over me in that moment will stay with me always. When they announced my name, so many memories and images came flooding back to me ... the moment I made my decision at age 15 to become a world champion ... the tender scene of my Tata presenting his love and faith to me ... the dismay of being homeless and broke ... all of the aches, pains, hard work and hope along the journey. I was finally at my destination. It was an incredible arrival and I still think about it with excitement in my heart.

World Champion Master Marco Sies

Marco Sies has trained in martial arts for more than 20 years, including full-contact kickboxing, Muay Tai, Karate, Shotokan, Gojuryu, Tae Kwon Do, Hapkido and professional boxing. These are some of his many professional accomplishments:

1992 — WAKO Featherweight Chilean National Professional Kickboxing Low Kick
Champion

1997 — IKC Featherweight Professional Kickboxing Champion
KIKA Lightweight Professional Kickboxing Champion

2000 — USKBA Super Lightweight Professional Full-Contact Kickboxing World
Champion

2002 — WWKF Lightweight Professional Full-Contact Kickboxing World Champion
Awarded 6th Degree Black Belt in Tae Kwon Do by the World Martial Arts
Organization
Awarded 6th Degree Black Belt by Grand Master Jonas Nunez, PKF President
Awarded 6th Degree Black Belt by Grand Master Keith Nesbitt, WWKF President

2003 — PKF Lightweight Professional Full-Contact Kickboxing World Champion

2004 — WPKO Lightweight Professional Full-Contact Kickboxing World Champion

2005 — KICK Super Lightweight Professional Full-Contact Kickboxing World Champion
USKBA Lightweight Professional Full-Contact Kickboxing World Champion

2006 — Awarded 1st Degree Black Belt in Hapkido by Grand Master Jin Pal Kim

2007 — Awarded 7th Degree Black Belt by Grand Master Jonas Nunez, PKF President

Halls of Fame and Other Honors

2002 — Inducted into the Karate World Hall of Fame as a Kickboxing Legend

2005 — Honored with Official USKBA Trading Card

2008 — Inducted into the World Professional Martial Arts Organization Hall of Fame
at Madison Square Garden as Master Instructor of the Year

Marco has also coached five amateur world champion kickboxers, as well as three international titleholders and three U.S. national champions. He is a master karate instructor and partner in Kicks Karate in Potomac, Maryland.

In the following years, my belief in myself became so strong, I went on to train with the Sugar Ray Leonard team and eventually won six other world champion titles. In 2005, I retired from the ring, turning my focus to instructing and helping others, opening the Kicks Karate school and training center with more than 500 students in Potomac, Maryland, in 2006. Our emphasis is on development of the mind, with the goal of teaching our students not only to be successful at the martial arts, but also to learn the principles of success and be confident in life in general.

Helping Others through My Experiences

Over the years, I have since found success as a martial arts grandmaster (one of the youngest at the time), became a hall of fame inductee and a successful business owner as well. Through the principles and essential elements I share with you here in *The Master Method*, I achieved success, not only in the ring, but also in other aspects of my life. I now understand that we all benefit through our challenges. Because of this understanding, I am able to face new challenges more positively and effectively and recognize the benefits of each more quickly.

My experiences have led me to the life I am privileged to have today, giving me the necessary tools and belief in my own powers ... not only to create success in my finances, my career, my health and relationships but, most importantly, to enjoy true happiness with my family.

I love my life, and every day I find new reasons to be happy and energized about the future. When a new challenge comes my way, I receive it humbly, with gratitude and open arms, knowing it will undoubtedly lead me down new roads of discovery. I can finally say I have left that self-doubting insecure little boy behind and found true peace within myself. I invite you now to explore the method I developed over the years — *The Master Method* — and apply it to your own life.

Why I Developed The Master Method

When I retired from fighting in 2005, I was offered an attractive job with one of the extreme fighting shows on television. Although it was without doubt a prestigious position with high visibility, I didn't considered it for even a minute. My fighting career never was about titles, money or fame — it was about discovering myself and being the best person I could be in whatever I pursued. *The Master Method* goes beyond philosophy and gives you a clear process for practicing the ideas of the ancient masters and modern teachers in your daily life.

There are plenty of self-help and motivational books and videos on the market. Many focus on success in business, achieving harmony between the sexes or between generations, how to improve family relationships or how to find inner peace. My goal with *The Master Method* is not only to inspire people, but also to show them how to become successful in *all* areas of their lives. I present my DCPC (Decide, Condition, Plan and Create!) Formula to share with you years of study and countless references, in a single book. *The Master Method* will give you the frame of mind needed to succeed, and it will guide you in maintaining positive thinking when faced with the roadblocks and barriers that inevitably present themselves. If I change thousands of lives with this book, or merely one life for the better, than I will have reached my highest achievement yet.

How to Use The Master Method

The Master Method contains a step-by-step formula and important exercises for implementing this proven equation for achieving success. No matter where you are in your life ... young or old ... poor or privileged ... whether you're hoping to make a complete change or simply a few improvements ... following *The Master Method* will help you appreciate and enjoy this one life each of us is given.

I'm well aware that everyone learns in a different matter. I'm sure there'll be those of you who quickly skim the book, take what you will and move forward. But as you read each chapter you will begin to understand how the circle of elements in *The Master Method* are intertwined to work together. You'll also realize the great importance of putting the exercises in the book into practice in your daily life.

As you begin this adventure of new thinking, you may find it helpful to refer frequently to sections of the book to remind you of specific points. Please note there are also many additional tools related to *The Master Method* at **www.themastermethod.com**. Over time, the ideas, concepts and exercises in this book will become second nature and, before you know it, you'll find *The Master Method* has become a way of life — a way of life that will lead you to your dreams.

What You Will Learn

The Master Method comprises a series of steps, called the DCPC Formula, which stands for Decide, Condition, Plan and Create! Using this formula, you will first *decide* what you want to achieve by acknowledging what you *don't* want and what you *do* want in the five areas of life. Next you'll learn the importance of *condition*ing your mind through gratitude, humility, positivity, faith in your plan and patience.

Step 3 shows you how to plan your journey with incremental steps to keep you moving along the route to your dreams. By the final chapter, you'll see how all steps of *The Master Method* work together to help you create success in all of areas of your life. We'll review the complete method and give you more essential tools and motivational tips on self-discipline, enthusiasm and breaking through barriers.

The DCPC Formula

Step 1: Decide	I *Don't* Want This / I *Do* Want That
Step 2: Condition	Conditioning Your Mind for Success
Step 3: Plan	Plan of Action
Step 4: Create!	Break the Barriers and Enjoy!

Your Journey Begins Now

Are you ready to open your mind and take control of your future? If so, you're about to embark on an exciting journey ... a journey to a life of peace, success, prosperity, joy and fulfillment — *your* life. It will be your ideal life; one you create, sculpt and feel proud of with each small accomplishment. Once you take control, you can achieve your goals, enhance your health, improve your relationships and, most importantly, strengthen your mind and your spirit.

No matter how many failures you may have suffered ... no matter how bad you feel physically, emotionally or both ... no matter how many unhappy relationships you've experienced or financial problems you've faced, this can be your new beginning. Even if you feel satisfied with your life already, *The Master Method* will guide you in making a good life great, or a great life even better!

Step 1: Decide

In the late 1980s, one of the greatest kickboxing champions of all time, Bill "Superfoot" Wallace, put on an exhibition in Santiago. For me as a young teen interested in martial arts, it was incredibly exciting to see someone of his caliber. I was completely awestruck and amazed at his talent. I was so inspired by his abilities, I decided at that very moment I wanted to become the world champion. From that day forward, it was all I could think about. I focused on that dream and everything I did in my life became part of staying on my path and working toward that goal.

Of course, when I shared my aspirations with my family, friends and even the martial artists I trained with, most of them told me I was crazy or made fun of me ... and some even laughed at me! No one even understood why I wanted to do this, much less support me by believing in my dream. Yet, somehow, I didn't allow their reactions to diminish my own conviction. I knew in my heart what I wanted to achieve, and I was going to do whatever it took to accomplish it.

It's All in Your Mind

We humans process tens of thousands of thoughts in our brains every single day. Some are passing thoughts that may not hold much significance, such as:

- What to wear
- The weather
- Which shoe to put on first
- Cereal or eggs for breakfast
- Good hair day / bad hair day
- How much coffee to pour into the cup
- Paper or plastic at the grocery store

And other thoughts seem much more significant:
- I hate my job
- I love spending this time with my kids
- How am I going to pay the bills this month
- My spouse is criticizing me again and I hate it
- When I volunteer at the hospital, I feel so happy
- I feel fat and I hate my body
- I don't know what to do with my life

We all process an incalculable variety of thoughts — small, insignificant, quickly passing thoughts, as well as sustained, contemplative and habitual thoughts — and it's impossible to be aware of and monitor every single one of them. But believe it or not, your past thoughts and feelings have created the situations and circumstances you're experiencing in the present, and you have the ability and power to shift your thoughts and feelings *now* to create a better future.

> **"All the breaks you need in life wait within your imagination. Imagination is the workshop of your mind, capable of turning mind and energy into accomplishment and wealth."**
>
> **—Napoleon Hill**

The Thought-Feelings-Energy Connection
It begins with a single thought. That thought produces feelings, and those feelings

produce energy. Energy — positive or negative — attracts more experiences and circumstances with similar energy. Thus, each person's current reality is the result of thoughts, corresponding feelings and energy produced in the past.

The thought process, either consciously or unconsciously, leads us to the creation of situations, circumstances, relationships and opportunities in our lives. Many people assume every situation and circumstance they face is random, based on luck or not within their control. So, they live their lives *reactively*, responding to random circumstances, situations and people, and consequently feeling powerless and at the mercy of fate.

> **"The universe, from its farthest galaxies, to its largest planets, to the tiniest particles in a single atom, exists as energy. Energy never stops. It's constantly changing from one form to another, and it's everlasting in time."**
>
> **—Master Marco Sies**

You Have the Power to Take Control

You have more control over your life than you think! Every thought that flows through our minds produces corresponding feelings, either positive or negative in nature. The feelings we are experiencing will result in energy around us, also positive or negative in nature, which will attract more people, circumstances and situations with like energy. And so, our feelings are the key to what ultimately manifests in our lives. And what controls our feelings? Our thoughts, of course.

Cognitive scientists believe at least 90% of all thought is unconscious thought, so in most cases, we are not even aware of our thinking. While most thoughts don't create strong feelings in us one way or another, others can produce strong and powerful feelings that will affect our energy, which in turn affects every situation and circumstance we encounter. So let's talk about energy.

Understanding Energy

Before we learn anything else about how to achieve a life of success, happiness, and true peace, and before taking the next step in our journey, we must first understand a little about this amazing universe in which we live. We are energy beings, as is everything around us. If we break down any living or non-living thing into its smallest particles — down to its molecules, atoms and even the smallest components of those atoms — we are left with the tiniest particles of constantly moving, vibrating energy.

We humans, when broken down into our organs, tissues and cells, can be broken down into smaller and smaller particles, down to our atoms, and those atoms can be further broken down into their components: protons, neutrons and electrons. The tiniest of these particles are in a constantly moving vibrational state, thus making every person formed by these particles in a state of vibration as well.

Like atoms attract each other. Like atoms vibrate with the same energy, and they bond to form larger particles. Those like particles compliment each other and attract more particles, combining even further to form larger and larger particles, and eventually forming non-living things or living beings. This attraction is the basis for everything that occurs in the universe, including everything that occurs in our lives.

When you, as a human entity, "vibrate" positively or negatively, through your thoughts, feelings, words or actions, you'll attract more of that similar vibration to your life. This attraction of similar energy and vibration could be in the form of people, situations or circumstances that will positively or negatively influence your life. Understanding this simple universal concept is the foundation for creating the life you desire.

You Are the Creator of Your Own Reality

YOU have the power to control how you are vibrating, positively or negatively. Therefore, the ability to bring whatever you want to your life is yours. You have the power to create your own wonderful reality, with faith that the universe is on your side. You'll hear me repeat this many times in my books, seminars and instruction sessions: *You are the creator of your own reality!*

By using *The Master Method* as your guide, you'll no longer be a passive spectator or victim of uncontrollable circumstances around you. You'll no longer reactively live a life of randomness and worry. You'll no longer have to hope or wonder if everything is going to turn out okay. Instead, you will develop into an active creator — an inventor of thoughts, feelings and positive energy that will elevate your state of being. You'll have faith that, whatever experiences you face, you're gaining wisdom and the tools to bring you closer and closer to your goals.

It's extremely important to realize your PAST thoughts and feelings have created the situations and circumstances you're experiencing in the present. Your current situation is the result of feelings you've already experienced, and you must remind yourself that those thoughts and feelings *are in the past*. They don't exist right now if you don't let them. More importantly, you have the ability and the power to create a new reality for yourself simply by shifting the way you think. This will change how you feel, and these new positive feelings will result in a positive shift in the people, situations and circumstances coming into your life. This is worth repeating: **You Are the Creator of Your Own Reality.**

So, as you read further and begin the exercises in this book, remember the importance energy plays in all you do. In order to construct the life you want in every area (career, finances, relationships, health and inner peace), you must pay attention to how you are "vibrating." What kind of energy are you emitting? Positive or negative? What are you attracting to your existence?

And so, to summarize: Thoughts alone don't possess much power. However, the *feelings* produced by those thoughts, especially strong feelings, possess the amazing power to change our lives. Those feelings are the key to creating our desired reality. By choosing to "vibrate" positively, we can create a positive reality and a truly amazing life.

The Power of Thought

Everyone talks about the power of positive thinking, but how exactly do we keep our thoughts positive? It would be a nearly impossible mission if we simply attempted to monitor all thinking. We have constant thoughts running through our brains day and night, and it would be an overwhelming task to try and keep track of them. However, paying attention to our sustained habitual thought processes would be one important indicator of how we are vibrating.

The easiest way to determine what kind of energy we are transmitting and attracting is simply to ask ourselves: *How am I feeling?*

Answering this most basic question can start to give you a clearer picture of the kind of energy you yourself are creating at this time in your life. Recognizing your feelings is very powerful, and if you find those feelings to be negative, don't worry, because it can all be turned around. Now that you understand the importance of the thought-feelings-energy connection, let's begin the actual work of changing some of your sustained habitual thought processes for the good!

I Don't Want This. I Do Want That!

Before navigating toward any destination, you need to know your starting point and then you can use your compass, map, instructions or GPS to help you get there. Let's begin the work by acknowledging what your current life's situation is and how you feel about each aspect of it. Mark the beginning of your journey by making a commitment right now to be an active participant in the process.

Write It Down

Your first action in this process of creating the life you desire will be to start a journal. You may wish to use *The Master Method Journal,* which will be extremely helpful in guiding you through the journaling exercises throughout this book or, if you prefer, any blank notebook or paper will work fine to write down your thoughts, lists and exercises. Whichever you choose, the writing process is *essential* as a highly powerful tool in preparing for a life of contentment and achievement.

On the first page of your journal, write a quick brainstorm list of answers to the following Starting Point questions. Read each question, then start writing immediately. Answer with the first thoughts and feelings that come to mind. There are no wrong answers and don't worry about how they're phrased. Your writings are for only *you* to see and evaluate, so it's extremely important to BE HONEST when answering these questions and others throughout your journaling process. The more honest you are, the more powerful this exercise will be.

EXERCISE: STARTING POINT QUESTIONS

Answer the following questions on page one of your journal. This first page will allow you to evaluate where you are right now in your life. Remember, brainstorm this list fairly quickly and be honest.

- What is the current state of my life?
- How do I feel about my life?
- What do I love about myself and my life?
- What do I NOT love about myself and my life?
- What are my feelings about where I stand in the following areas:
  - Career
  - Finances
  - Relationships
  - Health
  - Inner Peace

Once you've written all you can regarding the different areas of your life, and your feelings about your life, you now have a black and white, hard-copy representation of how you see your life now — your current reality. Believe it or not, this first page in your journal will be important in creating the life you dream of, especially if you wrote about areas in your life that you don't like, that give you stress or you wish you could change.

The Law of Duality

Recognizing and acknowledging the things in your life you don't like will be significant in your journey because of an important universal law called the Law of Duality or the Law of Opposites. This is the understanding that there is an opposite to everything, and that positive and negative give meaning to each other.

If there is an entity of evil, an entity of good exists as well. If you experience feelings of sadness, be sure you can also experience happiness as well. If you find scarcity in your life, the possibility of abundance also exists. Darkness and light, black and white, high and low, yin and yang ... opposites represent the perfect balance and counteraction of all the forces of nature and the universe, and this counteraction of opposite forces and their neutral balance is essential to the creation and sustaining of life.

In our lives, these contrasts allow us to appreciate one or the other end of the spectrum. Knowing that one extreme exists and having experienced that extreme allows us to understand and appreciate the other extreme. In addition, each opposite possesses the ability to change into its counterpart. As easily as we can experience one, it can almost as easily be transformed into the other. Because of this contrast, we can recognize and identify what we want in our lives. By looking at, feeling and experiencing the things we don't want, we are able to more easily recognize what we do want for ourselves in each of the areas of our lives:

- Career
- Finances
- Relationships
- Health
- Inner Peace

It's amazingly simple to take this first important step in turning your life around. In recognizing what you *don't want*, you'll realize what you *do want*. And once you know what you want, the next step will be learning to positively place your focus on THAT. And then the real fun begins!

EXERCISE: I DON'T WANT THIS/ I DO WANT THAT LIST
We are now going to *organize* the thoughts and feelings you brainstormed about previously, using the Starting Point thoughts on the first page of your journal as your guide.

1. Divide your next journal page into 5 sections:
- Career
- Finances

- Relationships
- Health
- Inner Peace

2. Under each section, using your brainstorm list as a reference, list all of the things in each area that make you unhappy, frustrated or bring you stress — things you would like to eliminate, change or improve. This is your I DON'T WANT THIS list.

3. On the following page, create your I DO WANT THAT list. Divide this page into the same five sections, and write a corresponding list of things you do want for each item you listed in your I Don't Want This list.

Example:

I don't want this	I do want that
A boss who is constantly criticizing me	A boss who is always praising me
Being overweight and out of shape	Being healthy, fit and at my goal weight
A relationship where I feel empty and sad	A happy, loving, peaceful relationship

In addition, on your I Do Want That list, you may add other things you DO want, even if they don't correspond to items on your I Don't Want This list. Think about what you are passionate about, what you love and what you really want for your life in each of the five areas. DREAM BIG! And don't allow your mind to limit you with thoughts of how you would achieve it, how much it would cost or how much training it would require, etc. **Just dream without limits!**

Note: The I DON'T WANT THIS list is especially helpful in the transformation

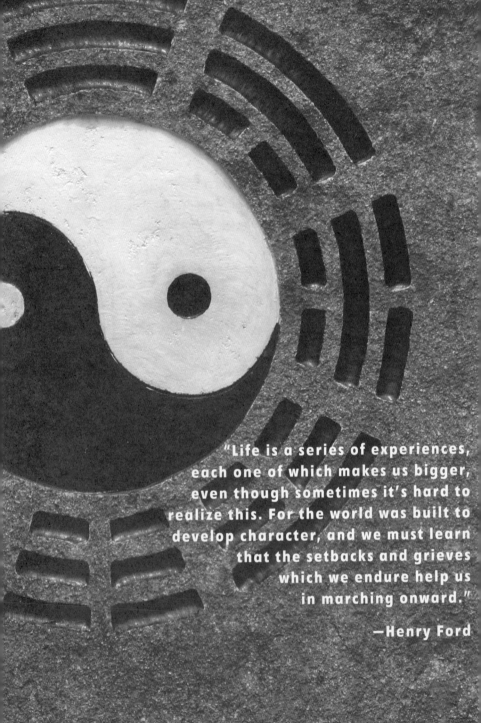

"Life is a series of experiences,
each one of which makes us bigger,
even though sometimes it's hard to
realize this. For the world was built to
develop character, and we must learn
that the setbacks and grieves
which we endure help us
in marching onward."

—Henry Ford

process because when we understand what we don't like, we will identify what we DO want by contrast. Then we can learn to place our focus on that and, as a result, turn things around!

Moving Forward and Releasing

What do you not like about yourself? What don't you like about your life? For some, formulating this list of answers could open up a floodgate of emotions and self-criticism. However, recognizing and acknowledging things you don't like in yourself and in your life is essential in the process of creating the life you want and becoming the person you'd like to become. The awareness of what we don't like allows us to realize what we don't want and, through the laws of duality or opposites, we can then identify what we do want for ourselves. Only then can we begin the process of shifting our focus to moving on.

Please keep in mind that, while recognizing and acknowledging what we don't want is a productive part of the success process. DWELLING on what we don't want so much that we generate and perpetuate an overall sense of negative feelings such as sadness, worry, anger, discouragement, frustration or resentment is not productive. You may experience thoughts such as:

- I hate not having enough money
- I can't afford things I really want
- I don't like the way she treats me
- I can't stand my job
- I hate my body, and nothing works to make it better
- If it weren't for him, I would be so much happier
- I am stuck in a life I can't change

Recognizing and acknowledging these thoughts and feelings are important. The next step, however, is even more important — MOVE FORWARD AND RELEASE THEM. Use these thoughts and feelings as a springboard to work toward and create what you do want for yourself. You can turn it around if you recognize that you can stop the cycle of perpetuating negativity, you'll be on your way to good things.

Negativity Attracts Negativity

Allowing our minds to sustain negative thoughts and resulting negative feelings only stimulates the attraction of even more experiences and circumstances with that same negativity. Negativity seeks and attracts more negativity. It's that simple. The more you dwell on what you don't want — think about what you don't want, talk about what you don't want, place blame on others for what you don't want, feel sorry for yourself because of what you don't want — and allow those negative views to bring about feelings of sadness, anger, frustration or depression, the more negative feelings and negative energy you produce. And, ... yes, you know the cycle: the more you will attract circumstances, situations and people in your life that match that harmful vibration.

You Can Break the Cycle

The negative cycle CAN be broken! That's the great news! The key to breaking the cycle is in understanding the vital concept I will repeat once again because it's so important:

Your PAST thoughts and feelings have created the situations and circumstances you are experiencing in your present, but you have the ability and power to shift your thoughts and feelings NOW to create a wonderful future.

You can begin to create a better future for yourself right now. You can begin simply by *positively* focusing your thoughts in order to **feel good**. This is another important concept I want you to always remember. If I had to leave you with only two words on a sticky-note to attract the life you desire, I would leave you with these two simple words:

Feel Good

How to Feel Good

Here's the prescription: Do whatever you can (in a healthy, positive way and within reason, of course!) to create good feelings within yourself.

- Think good thoughts
- Surround yourself with people you love
- Listen to good music
- Exercise
- Go to places you enjoy
- Participate in your favorite activities

By maintaining positive energy within yourself, you'll sustain positivity around you. As a result, this positivity will attract even more people, circumstances and situations matching that good vibration, which will multiply, giving you even more reasons to feel good. This will create a positive cycle of experiences and feelings that will move you forward on your path to achievement.

I realize that sometimes it can be difficult to maintain a positive attitude or sustain positive thoughts and feelings, especially when we experience challenges or unexpected turns in the road. Sometimes, as part of the path we take toward our goals, we experience situations we didn't expect or desire, although it may be part of a necessary set of learning experiences and tools we need to help us further along the way.

You're Only Human

Even the strongest in spirit can become weak and experience feelings of frustration, anger, despair or defeat. It's perfectly normal to have these feelings. And sometimes, we must allow ourselves these feelings of weakness in order to appreciate our contrasting wonderful feelings of strength. It may even boost our energy and motivation toward striving to maintain our positive feelings once they return. Don't forget, experiencing contrast reminds us of what we do want.

Choose the Positive Path

Do you remember the personal story of my first big American boxing match at the beginning this book? Some might have let that devastating event end a career. Of course I suffered feelings of disappointment, disillusionment, anger and failure as anyone would afterward. But I chose to move on, examine the situation and look for lessons to be learned and focused on that aspect, making it a positive.

The key is not to allow our low points to become SUSTAINED feelings of negativity. Walk yourself through those feelings and consciously make an effort to shift your feelings to a more positive outlook. There are always two choices you can make in every situation you encounter.

Example:

Negative Path		Positive Path
Focus on what you don't like about the situation	VS	Keep a clear picture in your mind of what you really want
Focus on what you don't want to happen	VS	Remind yourself how good it will feel to reach your destination
Dwell on how bad things seem	VS	Look for good in the situation, how it's strengthening you, how you'll benefit later
Feel terrible and blame others for your misery	VS	Focus on feeling good, despite the circumstance
Allow fears and worry to distort how you look at the situation	VS	Find an activity and change your focus to something that makes you feel good

Remember, there is *always* a seed of benefit in every situation we encounter, even if you can't see it immediately. With patience and time, it will come to light. So, just like in the old song, accentuate the positive — focus on what you want and choose to FEEL GOOD.

EXERCISE: FEEL GOOD LIST

Next in your journal, start listing thoughts, things, people and activities that make you feel good. It can be anyone or anything! Refer to this list whenever you need a boost of positive energy. Sometimes we need to actually remind ourselves to do the things we enjoy, appreciate the ones we love and allow ourselves time to shift back to a positive frame of mind and heart. Your FEEL GOOD list is personal to you, and *only* you can decide what to include on your list. An example of a Feel Good list is my own, which looks like this:

- Spending time with my family and playing with my children
- Spending time in nature
- Fishing
- Listening to my favorite music
- Watching *The Cosby Show*
- Teaching my students
- Meditation and prayer

The only one who can stand in the way of your success, and the only enemy you'll have to defeat on your journey, is *yourself*. Remember, only about 5 to 10% of the human mind is conscious thought, and the other 90+% is subconscious. These are thoughts and feelings, stored in our brains and based upon experiences from our past, even as far back as infancy. Some believe we are even affected by experiences prior to infancy. Every past experience and all of the thoughts and feelings associated with those experiences are stored in our subconscious minds, and we are not even aware of most of them. By making and referring to your feel good list often and choosing a positive activity, you can begin to create a positive mindset by feeling good.

Break Down Barriers by Feeling Good

If you were to travel back in time and observe your childhood experiences and interactions in detail, it would help you understand why your life is the way it is today, and why you think and respond the way you do in certain situations. Past interactions such as someone telling you you're not good enough or not capable, that in order to have money you must suffer or sacrifice, you can't do this, you can't do that, and so on, all influence how you think and behave now.

"Let the beauty we love,
be what we do."

—Rumi

Past negative experiences are the source of roadblocks and barriers preventing your success, happiness and peace. These experiences were imprinted on your subconscious mind, so even if you've consciously forgotten the details of thoughts, feelings and interactions associated with an event, they're probably with you today and will continue to have an impact unless you're able to identify them, understand them and change them. They'll continue to hold you back from realizing your dreams and achieving a masterpiece life, unless you condition yourself and your mind to turn it around.

Perhaps you never even tried to set goals for yourself because of past negative experiences and the belief that you were not capable, worthy or deserving. But now, you can change all of that and move forward toward the destination of your ideal life of success, prosperity, happiness and peace. In subsequent chapters, *The Master Method* will guide you in the conditioning process so you can break through those roadblocks and barriers, and this time you WILL follow through.

The Five Areas of Life

You're well on your way through Step 1: Decide of *The Master Method*. You've learned about positive and negative energy and the Law of Duality. You've identified what you don't want and what you do want. You've examined the power of thought and the thought-feelings-energy connection. We've discussed moving forward and releasing past experiences, as well as choosing the positive path.

In the next chapter, you'll learn to condition your mind for success, but before we go further, let's take a moment to look more specifically at the five main areas of life.

- Career
- Finances
- Relationships
- Health
- Inner Peace

Career

I find it interesting that so many people don't even know what it is they love or what it is they would really like to do. They live their lives just going through the motions.

Every day they get up, go to work and are on autopilot most of the time, doing what they're "supposed" to do, but hating each day. They complain about the job and the people they work with, they believe they are overworked and underpaid, and they just plain don't like being there and wish they were doing something else.

Identify Your Passion

If you're really miserable doing what you're doing, stop and allow yourself to think hard about what you would enjoy doing. Search deep within yourself and ask yourself what you truly love. What is your passion? As I mentioned before, dream without limits. What would you love to do, regardless of the requirements, the money or the circumstances? Just ask yourself without limitation, what would truly make you excited and happy to know you could wake up every day and do THAT?

Once you've identified what you would love to do, don't worry about how you're going to get there or how you are going to do it. When you get down about your current job, remember that it doesn't help to allow these bad feelings to continue. You ABSOLUTELY will not change your situation when you're focused on how unhappy you are. In fact, you'll be attracting more of those feelings and circumstances to you, virtually ensuring you really will be stuck there.

Shift from Negative to Positive

Now, after the few pages you've read here, you should be aware and realize that being stuck there will be *your choice* if you choose to continue to feel bad about it. Now, on the other hand, you can choose to shift your energy and begin to look at this job as a stepping stone for your next position, not as a sentence for life. If you choose to do your best in a positive manner, make the most of each moment and do whatever you can to create positive thoughts, feelings and vibrational energy within you and around you, everything will change.

From Fast Food to Fast Feet

One of my first jobs as a teenager in Chile was at a McDonalds. Was this my dream career? Of course not. But rather than focus on how hard the work was each day, I focused on my goal of becoming a world champion and I recognized this job as a stepping stone to a better life. So I tried to be the best McDonalds employee ever, knowing this was an important part of reaching my objective and creating positive energy. I read every employee manual. I tried to be the best at every task in the restaurant. I came in early and worked late, and soon was promoted to manager. I even won Employee of the Year! But the point is, whatever you are doing, be enthusiastic.

If you choose to visualize what you want, how you really see yourself with the job of your dreams — doing it, loving it and having the time of your life, whatever your current situation — you'll create positive thoughts, thus positive feelings. You'll begin to feel the excitement and the joy of being able to do what you love, and you'll vibrate according to the way you feel. This energy will attract everything necessary for you to create that reality — if you need to meet people, you'll attract them ... if you need education or knowledge, you'll attract that. If you're a good performer, and gain the attention of your employer, new opportunities can come your way. You can begin to attract everything needed for you to keep moving forward toward your ultimate career.

Finances

Of the five main areas of life, this is probably the area most people put at the top of their list of worries.

- Do I have enough money to pay my bills this month?
- How am I going to pay for this expense?
- Can I afford a new house, new car or college tuition?
- Will I have enough to retire? When can I retire?
- I wish I could just have enough to be debt free.

And on and on. The list of worries about finances can go on forever, and it seems to be a constant concern that never ends for most. My challenge for you now, as you read *The Master Method*, is to change your focus. Change your focus from the worry and frustration to focusing on what you really want. But the trick is HOW you do it. You're not truly changing your focus if you go from hating being broke to hoping to not be broke. You must totally shift your focus to the *opposite* of broke — abundance, wealth, prosperity!

At first, it may seem impossible, especially if you're trying to figure out how to put food on the table or cover your bills for this month. However, if you allow yourself to "play the game" with your mind, it will soon become easier to think this way and truly feel excited about it. It will soon become a picture you can easily paint in your mind and it will generate good feelings within you. And remember good feelings are always the goal. You want to generate positive feelings that you can sustain in order to keep your vibrational state positive.

Imagine your finances the way you would like to have them:

- How much money do you have in the bank?
- What does your life look like with the money you desire?
- What are you buying?
- Where are you traveling?
- How do you feel in your prosperity?

By imagining your financial state the way you want it — by playing it like a movie in your mind — you're creating feelings of excitement and happiness. These wonderful feelings will allow you to vibrate in tune with your desires, and you will begin to attract that reality to you. You'll attract all the people, circumstances and experiences you need to make financial abundance your reality.

Relationships

This area of life is the one that can affect the spectrum of every emotion we can think of in every way possible. Relationships can bring us to the highest of highs and the lowest of lows, more than any other area of our lives. The connection between two people is a wonderful thing, and it begins within each person. If you experience struggles within yourself or you're not at peace with yourself, it makes it very difficult to experience peaceful relationships with others. What happens around you is a vibrational mirror to what is happening inside. If you're having a problem with others, you must first look within yourself and "fix" what is going on in there.

The Blame Game

Most people blame external sources for their misery. Although an external source may be a trigger, YOU are responsible for allowing it to affect your emotions and for choosing which emotion you'll respond with.

Negative emotions:

- Anger
- Fear
- Resentment
- Jealousy
- Frustration

When you focus on negative emotions, you begin to vibrate negatively, so your circumstances will match that. If you continue with negative energy, you'll continue to attract more thoughts, feelings, people and circumstances to match and support the way you feel.

Similarly, when you focus on the negative qualities of another person you'll always find more things not to like, and it will be much more difficult to get along with anyone if you're focused on what you don't like. When you maintain this focus, you're not only making it difficult to get along in that relationship, you're harming yourself overall, by creating negative feelings that will begin to attract more negative circumstances in other areas of your life as well.

Finding the Good

When you focus on finding the good in another person, you'll attract more positive feelings. It will be much easier to get along with someone when you're intent on feeling good and paying attention to the good qualities he or she has. By doing this, you can surround yourself with positive energy, and the other person will see more good in you as well. It's important that YOU are in control of the way you feel, and not allowing external sources to control you.

Positive emotions:

- Love
- Gratitude
- Compassion
- Joy
- Kindness

By looking for the good rather than what you don't like, not only will you be able to understand the other person better, but you'll feel better and handle situations better in the event of a conflict or a disagreement. You'll also inspire the other person to feel better, and you can become the calming breeze for their emotional turmoil.

Never give in to anger, fear or any other negative emotions. You'll only make the situation worse. It's irrelevant whose fault an issue may be. The presence of any negative emotion, regardless of the trigger, will make it impossible for you to experience positive feelings. Your mind at any given moment can only experience either positive emotions or negative emotions — it can't experience both at the same time. So, by consciously exercising love, kindness, compassion, understanding, gratitude and joy, even in challenging circumstances, you'll be able to maintain a positive frame of mind and a positive vibration, which will translate into better relationships with everyone around you.

Health

The fourth area of our life is the area we tend to focus on physically. However, in order to truly enjoy good health, we have to understand that health begins in the MIND. As I have stated repeatedly (and I will continue to do so because it's so important!), we are energy beings ... we are constantly vibrating, either positively or negatively, depending on what we are focusing on. And because of this vibration, we are attracting more people, circumstances and situations that match our energy.

Examples of focusing on sickness:
- Being afraid of getting sick
- Being obsessed with germs
- Constantly talking about our ailments — aches, pains, illness, treatments
- Taking many different kinds medicine "just in case"
- Always reading or watching TV about illness, sickness and ailments
- Constantly worrying about whether each ache or pain could mean something terrible

For people who vibrate in this way, it's just a matter of time before they'll experience the types of physical ailments they're obsessed about not getting in the first place! At the very least, this way of thinking will prevent them from experiencing their maximum potential of good health physically, emotionally and spiritually. Vibrating in a "sickness or unhealthy-conscious" way will attract sickness to you.

Practice Good Health

That's right. It takes practice. Of course, it's important when you actually feel ill to seek medical help and listen to your doctor's advice. However, the quality and speed of your healing process will be greatly determined by the way you choose to think and feel during this process. Focus on feeling good; focus on health. Our bodies have the capability of healing themselves, and we have the ability to slow or speed our own recoveries.

It's very difficult for medicine and doctors to help a person whose predominant thoughts are negative in nature. I'm sure you know of someone who always seems to be sick, one illness after another... and if they're not sick, they're worried about becoming sick! They're constantly thinking about illness, all the while creating the perfect opportunity for it to manifest. Now, if you're that person, stop!

Once again, you are responsible for creating your own reality, so you can create a life of good health and fitness, simply by focusing on the positive.

Examples of good health thoughts and feelings:
- Feeling strong physically
- Feeling strong mentally and spiritually by experiencing peace, happiness, laughter and joy
- Attaining your goal weight
- Exercising regularly and enjoying it
- Repeating that you feel great and believing it!

You are creating your reality, so try to feel good right now. Feel the power of the universe manifesting through you. Get rid of those bottles or pills you really don't need, but have "just in case" and begin to create a healthy life. Even if you're experiencing illness or sickness right now, you can change that — not by negating medicine or by refusing help from doctors, but by changing the way you look at things, changing how you feel and changing your thoughts and focus to being strong and healthy.

Inner Peace

The last area of life is one that every person, without exception, seeks and yearns for. Inner peace is an experience of freedom — freedom from fear and worry, and freedom from the negative influence of destructive thinking. This freedom has its basis in the perfect balance between you and the universe. It comes from the understanding that you are not singular in this universe; you're a part of the whole and contribute vitally to its existence.

Understanding the Energy Centers

Human energy is believed to be stored and distributed through energy centers within the body. It's important that your main energy centers — Emotional, Intellectual, Physical and Sexual — are in harmony in order for energy to be used efficiently. If you shift too much energy to one of these centers, the other centers won't operate as they should. For example, if you're highly stressed, you may get bodily tired, even if you haven't done anything physical. It's a case of your Emotional center draining energy from your Physical center. Have you noticed that someone may get a bit grumpy or short-tempered after they've been studying hard for an upcoming test? That's because the Intellectual center has been zapping strength from the Emotional center.

Another aspect to achieving inner peace is having faith and really trusting that everything will go according to our intentions in the long run. We must know that all that's required is to feel good, no matter what the current circumstances are. Enjoy the journey and remember *you* are creating your future.

Taking the First Step

Suppose you got on an airplane, asked the pilot where it was going, and he answered, "Hmmmm, I don't know." Would you continue on to your seat and take that flight? Probably not. Similarly, would you make a trip by getting into your car and just start driving, without deciding first where you want to go? You may drive for a while, make random turns and end up in the middle of nowhere. Needless to say this would not be the most efficient way to take a trip, and it certainly is no way to live your life!

People are often amazed at the talents of experts throughout the world, amazed at their skill, speed, and precision in their craft. How do these experts perform with such speed and accuracy? It is very simple, and it applies to any expert in any field — surgeons, expert fisherman, award-winning chefs, and professional athletes — but it can apply to ANYONE. Anyone who excels or succeeds in anything has a crystal-clear vision of what they want to accomplish."

—Dr. Joe Kravitz

Where Are You Headed?
The first step in creating your ideal life is to DECIDE what you want it to be. Where do you want to go? When you don't have a destination and a clear picture in your mind, you'll either continue on in your current undesirable circumstances, or you'll wander aimlessly, ending up in random places and situations haphazardly. Or even worse, you could also end up being part of someone else's plan and living your life by default. If you know where you want to go, you can now take steps to prepare and move toward your destination.

Unclutter Your Mind
Sometimes it's hard to decide exactly where you want to go because your mind is filled with clutter from the past and present — what you have to get done on your to-do list or what you haven't done yet. And doubts can creep in: Am I even

worthy of where I want to go, or worthy of improving my life? Should I follow the path of my parents, my teachers or someone important in my life, even if I realize a relationship may have been unhealthy for me? Sometimes we seek to gain the approval of others and follow a path we think is expected by them, although it's not necessarily a path that feels right. Or you may have fear that won't allow you to attempt to improve your life — fear of failure, rejection, roadblocks or having to move out of your comfort zone and challenging yourself.

What's very important to realize is that ALL THE CLUTTER CAN BE OVERCOME if you recognize it's there — identify it, acknowledge it and consciously and systematically put it aside. In the following chapter, Step 2: Condition, you'll learn how to overcome clutter and roadblocks, and free your mind. The clutter can be cleaned out so it will no longer hinder your success. You'll be empowered to do whatever it takes to get to your destination, and there will be nothing to stop you anymore!

Find Your Passion

You may have several things you want to accomplish. But regardless, your first step is the same — you must first find your passion, deep within you by asking yourself what you really, really want. Sometimes you'll know the answer without hesitation. Other times you may have to go through a process of soul-searching and introspective evaluation to decide exactly what you want. Nevertheless, you must come to the point where you absolutely know without a doubt, with determination and emotion, what you seek to accomplish. And once you've answered this question, the next step will be the key to your success.

Visualization is the Key

Now that you've answered the question, "What do I really want?" you must picture it in your mind. Every day. Several times a day, close your eyes and form a clear image of what your accomplishment will look like. Form a literal mental picture. Have faith and really believe in the images your mind is projecting. You may even pretend it's your current reality. You must really feel this new reality and allow yourself to sense the happiness, joy, satisfaction and excitement of attaining your success.

Visualization is essential in *The Master Method* for success. By visualizing success, you'll be creating a vibrational match in accordance with your desires, and by this you will begin to attract people, circumstances, situations, experiences, and even knowledge that match your vibrational state. You'll attract the things you need to make your desires a reality and achieve happiness and balance in all areas of your life.

I was first exposed officially to the concept of visualization when I was young, perhaps 14 years old, while attending a philosophy school called the Samuel Institute in Santiago, Chile. One day, our instructor asked us to get into a comfortable position and, through very slow breathing, quiet our minds and relax our bodies. He then asked us to visualize a goal we wanted to accomplish. At this moment, I felt the greatness and the power within me. I felt happiness and joy, and I realized we are the architects of our own lives — we are capable of creating our own reality. It was then that I truly understood we have to be able to see success before we can experience it.

Practice Makes Perfect
In order to create positive feelings of excitement and anticipation, take a little time every day to visualize what you want to become, what you want to do, what you want to acquire — the house you want, the career you want, the relationship you wish for, the money you desire. Relax your entire mind and body, and focus your thoughts on your goal. Feel it in your hands. Smell it. Listen to the sounds. Taste it. Experience it in your mind. Make it a reality in your mind at that moment. At the end of this chapter, there's an exercise for this crucial part of the process of *The Master Method*. I'll guide you through a simple and easy meditation. I'll also describe a couple of exercises you must follow conscientiously, as they are significant steps in mastering success.

Visual Stimulators
That said, it's not enough just to think about success. You must feel it with your whole being and vibrate in alignment with your vision of how you want your life to be. When I decided I wanted to be a kick boxing world champion, I worked extremely hard to physically develop myself into that champion. I knew it would

take time, discipline and extra-human effort, but I could see it, I could feel the hot lights, I could smell the sweat, I could hear the crowd cheering. On the walls in my room were posters of champions I admired. I surrounded myself with the greatness I desired. Every morning, every afternoon and every night I saw the pictures of those champions and, in doing so, I was unknowingly reinforcing my visualization exercises. Every time I looked at those images, I felt optimistic. It renewed my energies. I got recharged with joy and happiness.

Whether your goals are huge, life-altering aspirations or lesser daily things to accomplish, the universal laws, principles, essential elements and steps you need to follow in order to achieve them are the same. These principles are quite simple and, over time, will result in inevitable success as long as they're understood and followed faithfully.

It's Time to Decide

Are you ready to decide with certainty, where you want to go? And once you decide, are you committed to actually doing it! It's not enough to just make the decision that you want something. And reading this book won't help if you don't take action. *The Master Method* was written to guide you in achieving your own personal success, not just by giving you concepts to read and experiences to relate to, but by guiding you through your own journey of implementation so you WILL reach your destination.

In the next chapter we talk about conditioning the mind. With each chapter you read, allow some time for introspection and to really think about how what you've read relates to you and your own personal situation. Start meditating and visualizing your goals. Write in your journal, and read what you've written as often as possible.

If you wish, write down more than the exercises suggested here. Put down on paper your thoughts throughout the process — your dreams and your plans. Draw pictures, cut and paste photos — anything that comes to mind. As I said before, the act of writing things down and reading what you have written is exceptionally powerful, and a vital action step in keeping your thoughts and feelings positive and making your dreams become reality.

Once you're able to DECIDE and form that clear picture in your mind, your thoughts, feelings, actions and energy will be positive and focused toward achieving the life of your dreams. You'll be amazed at the power of taking this very first step on your path. You'll feel a sense of excitement, anticipation and happiness that you have begun your journey to success.

EXERCISE: DETAILING YOUR 'DO WANT' LIST

Some individuals have a very clear picture of what they want to accomplish, so it's easy for them to create and describe images in their minds. For other people, it's a little more difficult to determine what they want, articulate their desires or form images of those desires. They might know they want a better life, but they don't know exactly what to do to make it better. Many times they just don't like their present state of affairs and they think that's just "how it is" or they don't feel worthy to live a better life. Sometimes they don't feel entitled to be at peace with themselves or in harmony with the world around them. This book—and even this very first exercise—can completely change those perceptions of feeling lost, confused or undeserving.

In your journal, try to describe IN DETAIL how you would like things to be in each of the five areas of your life — career, finances, relationships, health and inner peace. Using your I Do Want That list from the previous exercise as your guide, begin to add more and more detail to your descriptions so you have the most vivid picture possible of your future. At this point, you might even dedicate a separate page for each area, to allow for as much detailed description as possible.

This is where you can have some fun! Go ahead and describe your dream-life in detail: colors, sounds, smells, sensations, interactions, what you're wearing, how you look, etc., because these written details will help you create visual details in your mind when you meditate and carry out your visualization exercises. The more detail you can imagine, the easier it will be to generate those positive feelings that will create the energy you need to attract good things to your life.

EXERCISE: VISUALIZATION MEDITATION

Using your detailed I Do Want That list and descriptions you wrote for each of your five life areas, the following exercise will now take you to that place and allow you to experience your goals in your mind through visualization. This exercise should be repeated as often as possible so you can constantly create positive feelings of anticipation, happiness and excitement within yourself.

Find a place that makes you feel physically comfortable and relaxed. It may be someplace quiet, a favorite chair, your bed, the backyard or even a nice hot bath. Choose a place where you can take a few minutes to reflect — a place where you can be in connection with the inner you, with no distractions from the outside world. Even if you're not able to get to your favorite place, you can do this anywhere — your desk at work, parked in your car (never while driving, please) or in a waiting room. Wherever it may be, the important thing is you're taking a moment to focus your mind and your thoughts by following these steps:

- Sit or lie down and just enjoy the peace and harmony of being alone.
- Take a moment and close your eyes.
- Slowly breathe in through your nose, fill your lungs and slowly exhale through your mouth. Very slowly.
- Relax your body and quiet your mind.
- Regardless of your present state of affairs or what you were doing a moment ago, take all of those thoughts out of your mind.
- Forget your list of things to do or worries you may have.
- Empty yourself from logical thought and from feelings of your current life.
- Empty yourself of all preconceived and limiting ideas of what you can do or what you can't do.
- Now, imagine yourself empty and open, and fill that openness with the images, sounds, smells and sensations of the kind of life you want to live.

- Imagine each of the areas of your life exactly the way you wrote about them in your detailed description. Focusing on one area at a time, paint the picture in your mind: Career... Finances ... Relationships ... Health ... Inner peace.
  - Where are you?
  - What are you doing?
  - What are you wearing?
  - What sounds do you hear?
  - Who are you interacting with?
- Allow yourself to feel the satisfaction, excitement and joy of being in the profession you love and worked successfully toward. Allow yourself to feel the happiness of wealth and abundance. Feel the love of the significant person in your life and how wonderful it is to be in tune with each other. Feel the accomplishment of reaching your goal weight and being more physically fit than you've ever been. Feel the absolute peace and contentment from deep within yourself and the joy of knowing you can endure anything because of this peace.
- Remember, it's crucial to be VERY specific with the details in your visualizations. These details help to create a clear picture in your mind and, as a result, allow all the positive feelings to emerge — the feelings of reaching your goal. These feelings will in turn create the energy that will attract the people, experiences and circumstances necessary to allow you to actually make it a reality.

The most important aspect of your visualization process is creating with your thoughts the feelings that are going to attract all positive experiences of your life. The goal is to feel good at all times. If negative thoughts take over your mind, refer to your own writings and feel good about the outcome of your efforts. Stay focused on what you want, rather than what you don't like about your present situation.

"Ask, and it shall be given to you; seek, and ye shall find; knock, and it shall be opened unto you ... for everyone that asketh receiveth; and he that seeketh findeth; and to him that knocketh, it shall be opened."

—Jesus

Surround Yourself

What also helps in the visualization process is posting pictures, symbols and reminders of what you want to accomplish. A photo representing your dream job, a place you would love to visit, the house you dream of or the financial status you would like to achieve. Write a check to yourself for the amount of a paycheck you'd like to receive. Post these things in a place where you can see them everyday, and when things don't feel good or you're experiencing other types of negative emotions, refer to your writings and visual reminders. All of these small things can help to steer you back to a positive state of mind so you can continue attracting all the things you want.

Note: *If you'd like more help with visualization, go online to www.themastermethod.com, and visit the free download section of the website. With the following exclusive code you can download a free audio exercise guided by Master Marco Sies.*

Use code: wc2000ms

Let's Move On

I hope you've made the decision to move forward with actions and, by now, you should be feeling eagerness and excitement at your future prospects. Now that you've looked at your present situation, thought about what you don't want and what you want, have written it all down and created a picture in your mind of your ideal life, it's time to fully condition your mind to keep you on the path to success. Let's begin chapter two!

"In order to think positively, you must condition your mind through life-long practice."

—Master Marco Sies

Step 2: Condition

Now That You've Decided

Good! You've finished the first chapter of *The Master Method* and made a strong start on the path to achieving your goals. That was the first of four steps in the DCPC Formula. So far you have:

- Taken an insightful look at your current situation
- Made a list of what you don't want and what you do want in the five areas of your life
- Learned how thoughts invoke feelings, which produce negative or positive energy, meaning you are the creator of your own reality
- Explored some of the ways to create positive energy around you
- Discovered the value of visualization in forming a precise picture of your desired destination in your mind

Conditioning Your Mind for Success

In this chapter you'll be introduced to the concept of conditioning your mind, just as an athlete conditions his or her body for a race, a match, a fight or other sporting event. I do realize it's sometimes easier said than done when someone tells you to just feel good or think good thoughts or stay positive. Often our intent and desire are there and we really want to feel good, but soon we find ourselves back in a negative frame of mind and feeling not so good. No one wishes to think negatively or feel bad, and no one intentionally tries to do so. But all too often it has become a habitual way of thinking and being, and this is the cycle that must be broken.

That's All Well and Good, But ...

It's easy to feel good and think positively when things are going well. But in order to feel good and maintain a positive frame of mind in the midst of challenges and circumstances we may not like or anticipate, it requires a conscious conditioning of the mind. In much the same way we condition our bodies through exercise and a healthful diet in order to build strength and endurance, or simply to remain healthy, there are also ways of conditioning our minds for strength, endurance, health and, most importantly, inner peace. Conditioning our minds and finding true serenity within us is in itself a success. However, achieving success in every area of your life can become limitless once you've achieved inner tranquility by practicing CONSISTENTLY to condition your mind.

You Can Change Your Thinking

In order to maintain strength, endurance and health in our mentality, we must make this conditioning a life-long practice. Just like anything else in life, there is no magic light switch or overnight success potion to achieve success. The consistent and daily conditioning of your mind is the key, and must become a way of life — not something you practice for one day or week and expect results from. But if you're willing to learn, I promise you'll find these techniques do become second nature and the positive attitude you create will pay off in every aspect of your life.

Once you understand and incorporate the essential elements of conditioning your mind, you will always possess the tools to overcome your roadblocks, barriers and fears. Some of your barriers may be obvious challenges or situations you need to overcome. Other barriers may root deep in your subconscious mind, originating from neural pathways —nerve tracts that connect one part of the nervous system with another and are critically important in learning — formed in early childhood or perhaps even before that, and you're not even aware they are there. But with constant, consistent conditioning, your psyche can emerge strong, healthy and ready to face any challenge.

The Essential Elements for a Positive Mindset

As part of *The Master Method* to achieving success, I have compiled a list of essential elements that are not only vital for the attainment of success, but these components will allow you to create a life of inner peace, joy and happiness. Understanding, practicing, and making these elements part of who you are will allow you to create the ideal life you deserve.

As you read further, I will explain the importance of each of these elements, as well as share valuable exercises and practical ways to not only understand the elements, but also allow them to become second nature. By consistently practicing the conditioning exercises, remaining conscious of the essential elements and consistently reminding yourself to maintain or shift your mindset in a positive direction, a successful mindset will become a part of your being. You'll naturally think and feel positively, and success will become your new way of living.

The following is the list of essential elements for conditioning our minds to maintain a higher plane of existence. When we achieve this higher state and sustain thoughts and feelings consistent with each of these elements, we allow ourselves to vibrate positively and surround ourselves with positive energy. As a result, our paths begin to illuminate, and the creating process of our lives flows more easily. Now, you may be expecting these elements to be along the lines of self-confidence, persistence, discipline, vision, willpower, resolve, assertiveness and other characteristics usually associated with the subject of success. But I think you may be surprised by the essential elements I've used to condition my mind for success.

The Essential Elements for Conditioning the Mind
- Gratitude
- Humility
- Positivity
- Faith
- Patience

In the following pages, each of these elements will be discussed in detail and I will share exercises that will develop and enrich each of these qualities within you.

Essential Element #1: *Gratitude*

I've been teaching martial arts for more than 20 years now, and I'm often asked, "How do you do it?" People want to know how I am able to make each class an exciting class with enthusiasm and high energy, all day, every day. Even when I have a challenging group, with students that may be a little more difficult to teach, I see a great opportunity to become a better martial arts master. I feel grateful and remind myself of this gratitude every day. Maintaining energy and enthusiasm despite the challenges makes me a better instructor. Not giving in to what may be a frustrating situation or struggling student and creatively rising above the difficulties to stay enthusiastic and positive gives me a sense of accomplishment and satisfaction in every class. And for that, I'm extremely grateful.

Reminding myself before each class that I am grateful for being a martial arts instructor, keeps me in a positive frame of mind to lead the best session possible. I try to maintain a level of enthusiasm as if the next class were the last opportunity I may ever have to teach. The students deserve that and I feel privileged to give them my best. I am grateful for the challenges because they increase my knowledge, strength and ability to strive for improvement in becoming a better master, instructor and person.

A Powerful Emotion

Gratitude is a surprisingly powerful emotion that elevates your state of mind. As I have said before, and will repeat again, this higher state of mind will provide you with incredible strength and the positive energy to influence all the events in your life. Even if you encounter problems, seeking the seed of benefit and feeling grateful despite those challenges will keep positive vibration swirling around you and this energy will in turn result in more beneficial experiences coming your way.

Sure, there will be times when the unhealthy part of your mind will tug at you, and you may find yourself seeing the negative side of things, thinking about how much you dislike something, dwelling on how difficult a task is and all the reasons you can't and won't succeed. You're certainly not alone in these kinds of thoughts and feelings, or in finding yourself behaving in a way you wish you could change.

We All Face Barriers

As I mentioned previously, for a wide variety of reasons, we have a certain amount of clutter personal to us in our minds. And we all have circumstances from the past that challenge our way of thinking and pull us down a path of negative thoughts and feelings. You may have had parents who criticized or discouraged you. You may have had hurtful childhood experiences — physical or emotional — that made you feel fearful or undeserving. Perhaps you grew up in a financial struggle or in an environment immersed in negativity. All of your experiences early in life programmed you to think, behave and react to experiences in a particular way. You may have even had a very positive childhood but, for whatever reason, you continue to struggle with following through on a plan for success. Maybe you have trouble taking action and sustaining your momentum toward your goal.

A lifetime of experiences contributes to blocking your successes. Individuals manifest their mind clutter in different ways (fear, anxiety, indifference, procrastination, not taking action because the task seems too difficult), but it all basically boils down to this:

Sustained negative thoughts and feelings will prevent us from progressing down the path to our goals.

We all have some type of mind clutter from personal development that can pull us into a sustained negative frame of mind. This clutter must be cleaned up in order to achieve the life you desire. But, there is good news! These barriers can be overcome. In fact, just the ability to catch yourself falling into any negative thinking and recognizing the negative impact of sustaining this type of thought is a huge step in overcoming and conquering this unhealthy habit. The duality of knowing what you don't want contrasted with what you're striving to become often increases the motivation to get there, as well as the desire to feel the appreciation and excitement of the accomplishment once you do get there. Practicing gratitude is a particularly effective device in overcoming the barriers of negative thinking and mind clutter.

Rehearse, Rehearse, Rehearse

For some, gratitude is not a quality that comes naturally or easily, and for these individuals, the mindset of gratitude must be practiced. The more you repeat thoughts of gratitude, the more you'll actually experience feelings of gratitude, and the more you'll vibrate positively and attract positivity, which will start the constructive cycle all over again. By practicing thoughts of gratitude, eventually gratitude will become an emotion from your heart automatically, and it will become a part of who you are deep inside. The more you practice thoughts of appreciation and gratitude, the more you'll find to be grateful for.

My Daily Gratitudes

Every day when I wake up, I practice my visualizations. This is a process I have used since I was a teenager, where I intently focus on how I want my life to be. I visualize even to the smallest detail, the images, smells, sounds and feelings of how I desire the parts of my life to be. When I'm projecting these images and desires, I always feel a sense of gratitude, even though the realization of that desire has not yet come to be. I create the thoughts and feelings in my mind, and I even feel the emotions in my body as if it were already a reality. I smell it ... I listen to it ... I feel it in my hands ... I hear the sounds ... and I feel grateful for that moment and for the experience. I feel the excitement of being there, even if it is only in my mind for now. Then, after I come out of my goal visualization, I place my focus on what I am already grateful for — my current life and all of the blessings I am receiving.

Recognize and Acknowledge

This is a central part of the process of conditioning your mind — the recognition and acknowledgement of the things you are grateful for in your current situation. It can be your kids — their smiles, laughter or funny things they do ... a relationship — how much you love that person and how he or she enriches your life ... having a roof over your head — this in itself is something to be grateful for, when you realize how many don't even have that ... having food to eat — remember how fortunate we are in the small things we take for granted ... your job — just having a job in recent times is something to appreciate given how many have suffered as a result of the weak economy... your health — many take this for granted as well, but we should all be thankful for each and every day we spend on this earth.

And so, you see, when you focus on what you're grateful for, you automatically begin to feel good. Use what you already have to create a positive frame of mind and remember, when you feel good, you vibrate in alignment with the life you want. You'll start attracting all of the people, situations and circumstances to get you there.

EXERCISE: THE DAILY GRATITUDES

When you wake up in the mornings, make it a habit of citing all the things you are grateful for. You can do this before or after you your visualization exercises, or any time throughout your day. Make it a practice you do as often as possible. Our minds are churning constantly, so why not fill them with beneficial thoughts of gratitude. Strive for gratitude to become your natural way of thinking and feeling. At first, you may need to make a conscious effort in remembering this exercise. You may even need to write a daily to-do list of things including *remember all I am grateful for*. In time, the conscious exercise of listing these gratitudes will evolve into your entire outlook. You'll naturally seek the good in any person or situation and feel gratitude for his or her existence. You'll eventually possess the ability to instinctively recognize and feel thankful for even the most challenging people and situations, because you know they're strengthening you and gaining helpful tools to reach the goals and life you desire.

Write a new daily gratitudes list in your journal each day. At the top of your list, start with what you're most grateful for today — family, friends, your work, your health, all of the things you enjoy and the things that are going well. Be grateful for everyday things ... for a beautiful sunrise or sunset ... for being able to see, hear and experience this wonderful world. It might be as simple as a friendly

"The voice of wisdom cannot be heard, except to the ears of an empty and humble mind."

—Master Marco Sies

waitress at your favorite coffee shop, or time for a short walk on a sunny day. Be grateful for your mere existence and for being able to experience all life has to offer. Be grateful now, with the faith that you'll receive what you are seeking. Feel the excitement of waiting for it and know it is coming.

When Things Aren't Perfect

Sometimes, however, you may have to be creative when looking for daily gratitudes. For example, you may not be in your dream career position right now. In fact, you may not even enjoy your work right now. But if you allow yourself to be thankful that this job is ultimately helping you gain experience or is serving as a stepping-stone or means of support to get to your ultimate career, then those positive thoughts will allow positive feelings to flow. Write those things down in your list.

We all have bad days, and on these occasions it's especially important to feel grateful that you have the opportunity to grow, gain strength and receive tools to become what you want to become. Feel thankful that you're preparing to receive what you want, and you're continuing to create your ideal life just the way you want it. As you learned earlier, every experience — good and bad — has a purpose and a benefit. Remind yourself of this every time you face adversity.

So, look for things to be grateful for. Think about them often. Sense the positive feelings resulting from those thoughts. This will help you stay on the right path and keep you in the highest state of mind possible.

Essential Element #2: *Humility*

Imagine for a moment you wanted to climb Mount Everest. Right now, you're wearing shorts and a t-shirt. You have not researched, trained or prepared in any way, and you have absolutely no climbing equipment or cold weather clothing. It would be extremely difficult for you to survive a journey like this if you left unprepared. You must learn to climb, train, get the necessary clothes and tools, and perhaps gather a team of individuals to help get you there. You may have to face some challenges while you acquire the necessary knowledge and physical

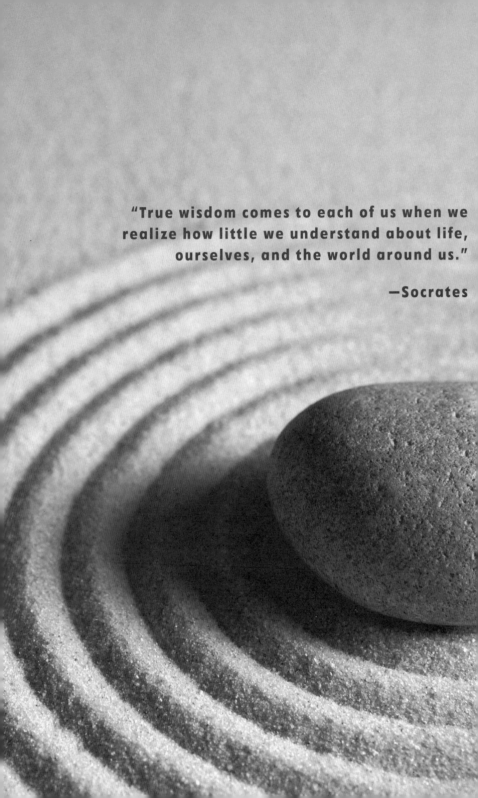

"True wisdom comes to each of us when we realize how little we understand about life, ourselves, and the world around us."

—Socrates

training, but you keep your ultimate goal in mind and do whatever it takes to reach the summit. In this scenario, you humbly accept the challenges as necessary experiences that are giving you the tools to become stronger and more equipped to face the climb ahead.

Likewise, when you're heading for a destination of success in life, every situation you encounter is either teaching you something you need to know, or giving you the insight or understanding you need to endure tests along your journey to success. Humbly accepting every experience as beneficial will help you remain in a positive frame of mind, even when you face disappointment or defeat. Remain humble and accepting of every situation as it presents itself. Avoid feeling resentful, defensive or angry about challenges and roadblocks. It's much better to move forward constructively, rather than trying to place blame or dwell on the negative.

The Silver Lining is Real

There is always a benefit or opportunity in every circumstance you face. Look for it! The benefit can come in many different forms. It may be strengthening you spiritually, developing your character or it could be teaching you how to effectively deal with hardship or misfortune. These are all instruments that will help you in later steps on your journey. Maintain a sense of humility through rough patches so you can maximize your benefits from them. Humility will always contribute to your positive mindset and result in the positive vibration of energy around you.

Losing is Nothing More Than a Big Part of Winning

In some situations, you may feel as though you've "lost." Don't let a negative event or setback stop your momentum. Humbly accept it as part of the process, and remind yourself that you're becoming stronger, wiser and more equipped to continue on. Whenever you face a disappointment, just remind yourself that losing is just a part of learning to win. You will win in the end, as long as you don't give up.

How to Practice Humility

How can you practice being humble? Here are a few practical suggestions for ways to weave the virtue of humility into your nature.

"Negative thought and pessimism
are the most important
reasons of failure."

—The Dalai Lama

- Empty your mind
- Receive knowledge and help from others openly and with a fresh mind. You may learn something valuable that will help you later. Even if it's something you've heard before or think you already know, receive it openly, with gratitude.
- Take these kinds of thoughts out of your mind:
  - How difficult it is
  - Why it may not work
  - Reasons you shouldn't move forward
  - I don't have the money
  - I don't have the experience
  - I don't have the expertise
- Open yourself to every experience, good or bad
- Open yourself to receive the benefit of the experience
  - Actively look for the benefit and identify it
  - Allow yourself to think thoughts and feel feelings of gratitude for the experience

The first item on the list is particularly important. Before you even begin your journey, imagine you are emptying yourself of any preconceived ideas, negative experiences or anything cluttering your mind that may hinder the receipt of valuable knowledge. Take out of your mind all the reasons why something may not work or how difficult it's going to be. Nature will give you all the answers you need to accomplish your goal. Open yourself up to receive new knowledge presented to you, for these contain character-strengthening experiences and wisdom that will help you in the attainment of your goal. Allow yourself to receive and benefit from any information, so you don't waste a single opportunity or experience. Avoid at all costs the attitude that you already know everything you need to know or that you don't have room for another way of looking at things.

Be a Receiver

Imagine a glass of juice filled to the middle, and you try and pour another full glass of water into it. The glass of juice will overflow, and much of it will go to waste. There's not enough room for both the juice and the water. Humility is much like that — being humble (emptying yourself) allows you to make room for insights, perceptions and understanding. Being able to empty yourself, so when you fill your glass, you can keep every bit of valuable knowledge and not waste a single drop. Sometimes you may not immediately grasp the teachings of a situation, but don't waste the opportunity when it is shown to you.

Be humble. It will put you in an open, positive frame of mind that will allow you to advance toward your dreams with as few stumbling blocks as possible. Once you become receptive to the seeds of benefit in all circumstances, your path will become clearer with each life experience.

EXERCISE: LIST OF BENEFITS

In your journal, create a list of recent challenges you've faced. Now empty yourself of any negative thoughts or preconceived ideas about how this challenge affected you or will affect you. For each challenge, list as many benefits as you can that resulted or could result from this experience. What tools did you or could you acquire from this challenge?

Think very carefully about the positive effects of each challenge and how each situation could be beneficial.

Examples of benefits could be:
- Strengthening of your spirit
- Appreciation of something or someone who makes you feel good (the opposite of the challenging situation)
- Teaching patience
- The circumstance led you down a path toward a person who could benefit you in some way

Essential Element #3: *Positivity*

The third essential element in *The Master Method* for conditioning your mind for success is positivity. Positive thinking is the fuel needed for your desires to become reality. If we use the road trip analogy again, at this point in your trip, you've chosen your destination so you know where you're going. You're now preparing yourself so you won't get lost on your journey, and you want to get there in the most efficient manner possible. You have the vehicle to get you there, but you must have the right fuel to keep the vehicle running smoothly and efficiently, so you won't break down along the way.

The same is true to experience success in any area of your life — you must nourish yourself physically, emotionally and spiritually so you can avoid breaking down. While it seems somewhat easy to identify ways to remain healthy physically, it can be much more complicated to identify how to obtain and maintain emotional and spiritual health.

From the Heart

"Positive thinking" is a phrase that's been used and re-used so much we often forget what it truly means and how powerful it really is. Thinking positively is not just a superficial catch phrase we can lightly gloss over or a concept we can try for a minute, and then wonder why we get frustrated when it doesn't seem to be working. Positivity must become a way of life, despite difficult circumstances. It can't be demonstrated just in words and actions, but in feelings existing deep within our hearts. With true positive thinking, you can create positive feelings, which create positive energy ... and that energy attracts positive results.

Remember what we learned about the thoughts-feelings-energy connection? Energy is always vibrating, and we choose to vibrate either positively or negatively, according to the way we sustain our thoughts and resulting feelings. Reflective of the way we are vibrating (either positively or negatively), we attract into our lives, good experiences or bad experiences ... good results or bad results ... success or failure. The reality we create for ourselves begins with a single thought. That thought is the base that creates feelings, and those feelings are the power, with all of its vibrational energy, that influences everything around you including the people, situations and circumstances you experience.

You Can't Fool Yourself

Sometimes people think that by doing something nice, despite their true feelings of negativity beneath the gesture, they'll achieve positive results. The act of doing something nice for someone is great, but if deep inside you feel negative feelings, such as anger, jealousy or resentment, then you're not being sincere, especially with yourself. These feelings will only create more negativity, unless you can find a way to honestly feel good about your deed. Doing something thoughtful for another person is always a good thing, but it *really* makes a difference when you sincerely feel good when you do it.

Your True Feelings

Imagine yourself in a situation where you have to face something difficult, like a major setback in a big project, or something unexpected that wasn't part of your plan. For most people the first natural internal reaction is to feel bad, or experience fear or doubt. You then attempt to think positively and mask what you're really feeling by pretending to feel good. You tell yourself and others around you that you're okay. You tell them you're thinking positively, although deep inside, you don't actually feel that way. Although what you're saying on the surface is positive, your true feelings are those of fear, doubt, frustration and insecurity.

These true and deep feelings are what you're actually projecting into the universe and, since these real feelings are creating a corresponding negative vibe, ultimately you continue to attract negativity into your reality. All too often a person temporarily thinks positively, but is unable to sustain those thoughts and feelings the minute he or she experiences a disappointment. Subsequently discouragement spirals downward into feelings of worry, frustration, unworthiness and perhaps hopelessness or even anger.

How to Reset Your Default for Positivity

True positive thinking and feeling good has to become second nature, so you no longer have to consciously choose between thinking positively or negatively, or feeling good or feeling bad. Positivity and feeling good has to become your default way of thinking and feeling, and as a result you'll always attract good energy.

How can you accomplish this? Understanding the concept is a good start, but now you must master the process of *how* to achieve this quality within yourself. Most importantly, mastering the art of positive thinking and feeling good during difficult times is the challenge. It's easy to feel good and think positively when everything is wonderful. This is natural and effortless. However, when we reach a roadblock or perceived failure, it can send us into a tailspin from which it may be hard to recover.

Emotional Roots

Understanding the roots of your thoughts and emotions will be the key in overcoming these difficult times and achieving and maintaining a positive frame of mind, even when you're faced with difficult situations that challenge your positive state. Before you can eliminate negative thoughts and emotions, you must be able to understand them. Why are you experiencing them in the first place? What is the root cause? And always know the answer is within you.

The cause of your emotion is NOT the situation, or a person, or a particular circumstance happening outside of you. You allow yourself to feel negative emotions as a reaction to things happening outside of you. You always have the choice to feel the opposite emotion. If you're feeling negative, stop and analyze the feeling. Try to identify what within you is making you feel frustrated, angry, worried or hopeless.

- Are you afraid of failure?
  - Remember, failure is only a big part of success, so don't let temporary defeat get to you. Temporary defeat lets you know you need to tune up your plans, and it teaches you something or allows you to experience something necessary in order to become successful. As I mentioned before, feel gratitude for the knowledge and experiences presented to you, even if it appears as temporary defeat. Without it, your success would be impossible. When you experience a temporary defeat, keep the end result in your mind, no matter how distant it may seem. The timing of nature and the universe is not our timing, and success may be just around the corner.
- Do you fall into a habit of negative feelings because of repeated experiences as a child?

- Unfortunately, many of us experience negativity as a child — whether intended or not — in the form of discouragement from our parents, teachers, siblings or other children. Perhaps you were told you weren't smart, or you weren't attractive or you'd never make anything of yourself. Or maybe you were compared to a brother or sister, or simply ignored, making you feel unloved. These feelings of unworthiness can have a long-lasting effect on anyone, even if these experiences came at a very young age. The resulting feelings and self-esteem issues root deep within our subconscious minds and they can affect how we behave years and even decades later, without us even realizing it.

Diffuse Negative Tendencies

Don't repress or ignore the roots of your emotions. Allow yourself to recognize what you're feeling and really try to understand where it comes from. Only then can you diffuse its power. If you don't go through this process, these negative emotions will inevitably come back again — and even stronger. Ignoring our emotions is like blowing air into a balloon. Over time, emotions accumulate. They build up more and more and, eventually, just as a balloon would pop when it can't accumulate any more air, you'll reach your breaking point in an explosion of emotion.

Making the effort to consciously and consistently monitor the way you think and feel is fundamental in the process of understanding your thoughts and emotions. Once you're able to identify your thoughts and feelings and understand where they come from, you'll have the ability to eliminate the power they have over you and you'll choose to "walk through" those negative feelings. You choose to think and truly feel positive instead. You can now allow the healthy part of your mind to take over. With the ability to understand yourself, shifting negative thoughts and feelings will eventually become automatic, and positive thinking and feeling good will become second nature.

The Master's Way

The ultimate accomplishment is when you know no other way but good, inside and out. This is when you've truly mastered yourself. You've not only mastered your mind, you've mastered your true self, your essence. This is the place of true masters, and a place every being should strive for. Regardless of how long it may take, mastering yourself —your essence — should always be the goal.

The mere attempt and process of sincerely trying to master ourselves truly makes us better. The first step in the process is to master your mind — your thought process and the way you feel. As we've discussed, when you master your thoughts and you feel good, your interactions with others are positive. You possess enthusiasm that becomes contagious. Everybody wants to be around a person with eagerness and enthusiasm. They'll want to be around you because your positive energy makes them feel good. People will want to do business with you. Your colleagues will develop a trust in you and a loyalty to you. In their subconscious minds, they want to be part of your happiness and your victories, so they too can feel happy and victorious. So *choose* to feel good. *Choose* to show enthusiasm. These qualities are valuable fuel that will propel you more quickly along the path to your goal.

Don't Let Stumbling Blocks Trip You Up

In the process of accomplishing something, you may find yourself face to face with disappointment or difficulties. When this happens, you must not forget that all things you encounter are preparing you for the accomplishment you're seeking. Keep the end result in sight — your goal, your accomplishment. Don't allow setbacks to activate the unhealthy side of your mind by sustaining thoughts and feelings of frustration, worry or fear.

When disappointment or unpleasant things come your way, don't give in to your negative reactions. As soon as you feel them overtaking you, acknowledge them as unhealthy thoughts and feelings, recognize where they came from, and shift them. To shift your negative feelings to positive ones, make a conscious move from thinking about what you *don't* want to what you *do* want.

Find the good in every situation you encounter. Find the positive seed that's there for you to benefit from. Sometimes you'll see it immediately. Other times, you may not understand it for a while. But no matter how long it takes for it to appear,

"Every situation has the seed
of something positive that will
come out of it — a benefit of
equal or greater value to
the challenge you faced."

—Napoleon Hill

the seed of benefit is always there. It may be giving you the tools necessary to succeed in the next step of your journey to success, or it may be giving you knowledge that's needed to understand and master the unhealthy part of your thought process. Some situations may simply serve the purpose of showing you what you *don't* want, so you can identify and work toward what you *do* want more efficiently and effectively from that point forward.

Whatever You Look for, You Will Find

If you look at any situation, you may find good, positive and pleasant things, and you may find bad, negative and unpleasant things as well. Likewise, you'll find the same dichotomy with people you encounter in your life. You may see wonderful qualities and characteristics you love about them, and you may see their flaws and qualities you don't like. It all depends on what you focus on and the kind of eyes you're using to see them — negative eyes or positive eyes. What are you looking for and what do you choose to see?

In an excellent book, *Money and the Law of Attraction*, by Esther and Jerry Hicks, they explain that if you sustain a way of thinking for a period of seventeen seconds — a good positive thought — it will attract more thoughts with the same vibrational match. The positive thought will attract more positive thoughts, which will result in ten times the positive energy, thus attracting positive experiences with ten times the strength. In the same way, sustained negative thoughts and feelings create strong negative energy and negative experiences.

If you enter a situation or an interaction with a person with an eye for the negative, you will absolutely find everything negative and unpleasant about the situation or the person. Negative feelings will form within you, and this will in turn attract more negativity. It's a simple universal law.

Expect Good Things

However, if you choose to look for something positive and stay focused on that — regardless of the situation or the person you're dealing with — you'll be amazed at the outcome. Your choice to see the good in any person or situation will result in positive feelings within you, which will produce positive feelings and actions in the other person as well. Your choice to see the good will result in more good coming to you. By choosing to see the good, you'll be able to think good things and, most importantly, feel good. And feeling good will allow your dreams to become reality.

Dealing with Difficult People

Sometimes you may face extreme difficulty in recognizing what could possibly be good about a difficult circumstance or person you're dealing with. The unhealthy part of your mind allows you to wonder why in the world you've been placed in this dreadful situation, or why you must deal with this horribly difficult person. These are the times when you really must remind yourself to shift your thoughts and energy to a positive state, so you'll be able to receive all the good that's coming to you.

Focus on feeling good. Choose to not let this person or situation influence your thoughts and emotions in a negative way. YOU control your own mind and how you will react. Don't let a negative individual or interaction take control. Stay focused on positivity. After you step away from the confusion, allow yourself some time to cool down and let your mind return to a neutral state — a state where you're not angry, frustrated or stressed anymore. In order to do this, it is important to have a few minutes with no distractions, so your mind can really settle, and it won't have the opportunity to return to that negative state.

Hit Replay

When you find yourself more comfortable, replay the situation in your mind and consciously put into practice the concept of self-discipline. Don't let your mind go back to the negative state of anger or frustration. Empty yourself of judgment, and with all of the compassion in your heart, focus only on how you could have handled the situation in a more positive way. Imagine it vividly in your mind. Play it like a movie in which you are the director and the main character.

Take the Compassionate Road

Practice love, understanding and compassion. It's much easier to keep yourself vibrating in a positive way when you do. In fact, love is the highest, strongest and most powerful of all vibrations. Be sure you don't get distracted in this exercise and fall into negative judgment and allow yourself to return to an unhealthy frame of mind. It's imperative you practice self-discipline and not fall into negative judgment.

We are faced daily with people and circumstances that can challenge our peace and positive mental attitude. When dealing with a difficult individual, try and understand the underlying motives for his or her behavior — the real reason behind the words and actions. Perhaps he is ill ... or just received bad news — or maybe she has an unkind boss or difficult situation at home to deal with. When you have compassion, it's easier to think of how you could have handled the situation in a more positive way.

Project Composure

Practice will help you gain self-discipline in shifting your frame of mind from negativity to feelings of love, understanding and compassion. In this state, you're able to realize that the harmful words you are hearing comes from someone who doesn't know how much he is also hurting himself. Through your compassion, understand the person's pain and try to rise above the negativity by not giving in to anger and frustration. Don't let your ego control you. Even if you have to use strong words to deal with a situation, make sure you're calm inside, and project composure to the person in front of you. Try and become a calming breeze to him or her. Let her know you're not there to hurt her, but to help her succeed. This is an important step that can return both of you to a positive state of mind.

By taking this approach, you'll feel much better about the situation and heal yourself much faster. This will result in shifting your thoughts and feelings into a positive state now and may even help you shift to positivity sooner the next time you encounter a problem. Your mind will be stronger, and you'll be even better equipped to handle difficult circumstances in the future.

As you know by now, in every situation we come across, there is some seed of benefit — there is purpose. You're gaining knowledge about yourself, someone else, or about what your next step on your path should be. You may be gaining

"Anger and intolerance are the enemies of correct understanding."

—Gandhi

tools or strengthening your character or your spirit. And so you see, there is a reason to experience every situation because it's part of your passage to success.

EXERCISE: PLAY MOVIES IN YOUR MIND

Previously, you were introduced to the concept of visualization. Be sure to practice it, no matter how things are going around you. Every day, set aside some time to just close your eyes and relax. Find a quiet place if you can. If not, practice it wherever you are.

When you wake up in the morning, before you retire at night, and anytime you can find time throughout the day, close your eyes and focus again on what you want. Play it like a movie in your mind, and allow yourself to experience even the smallest details of how you want your life to be. Don't let your current circumstances or problems take your mind away from what you really want.

Have fun and enjoy your visualization. Don't forget, it's very important you allow yourself to feel good. Experience all of the elements of how you want your life to be so you can elicit good feelings within you. These feelings will allow you to begin vibrating immediately in tune with your desires and as a result, you'll begin to attract them! This exercise does not have to take long, but you must be consistent in your practice and make these exercises a habit.

After you finish, don't worry about if and when the things you visualize will materialize. Simply TRUST that you're attracting everything you'll need to achieve the life you desire, and the universe will find the most efficient way to get you to your destination.

Essential Element #4: *Faith*

In order to condition your mind for success, there are five essential elements you must weave into your fiber of being, and the absence of even one of them will result in either failure to accomplish your goals, or failure to maintain them for any period of time. And so we come to the fourth essential element in conditioning your mind for success — faith.

Once you've determined what it is you want and you project your thoughts to the universe, without the fourth essential element of faith, the vibration you're emitting to the universe is weak and unclear. It's somewhat like declaring you want something but not being sure you deserve it or can achieve it. If you know what you want with absolute certainty, you must completely believe you can accomplish it with every molecule of your being. You must have FAITH that success is coming.

Believe It to Achieve It

If you truly believe it, you WILL achieve it. And similarly, if you believe something is impossible or too hard to accomplish, and you have doubts, it absolutely will be unachievable. You must firmly believe you're on your way to accomplishing your goal. Only then can you successfully take the necessary steps to get there.

After accomplishing your first step of deciding with certainty what it is you really want, ultimately, your faith will determine if you'll realize your goal or not. I believe this is the most critical essential element needed to become successful in the accomplishment of *any* of your goals. "Faith" in this case, does not simply refer to a religious faith, although if your religious faith is true and pure, that will certainly help and can be combined with the essential element of faith we speak of here! The element of faith in conditioning your mind for success is the strong, unwavering and steady belief that, no matter what circumstances you're faced with, you'll reach your goal or anything in your life you desire.

Know It in Your Heart

It is not enough, however, to just believe you can do it. You must really KNOW without a doubt that you will do it no matter what! Faith is a deep-down belief that you will reach your goal, even when you experience challenges. Faith is also the acceptance of every experience — good and bad — as a necessary part of the process. It's effortless to have faith when things are going just as you planned. However, when you experience an unexpected turn or delay, if you face a frustrating situation, or you make a failed attempt at a task, this is when faith can be challenged. And this is *exactly* when faith is most important.

Receive everything that comes your way with faith that all you experience is leading you to your goal. Every experience is preparing you and teaching you. Every experience is providing you with the wisdom, strength and tools needed to reach that wonderful place—the place of realization of your desires and the accomplishment of your dreams.

Finding Your Faith

In order to maintain your faith in achieving success, empty yourself of all preconceived ideas of how hard an undertaking might be, thoughts of how you're not good enough or don't have enough money ... or any negative musings that could be blocking your success. It's particularly easy to find excuses as to why something won't work, why you're not progressing, or why you're not trying in the first place. All of these roadblocks and detours can challenge your faith that success will find you.

However, once you recognize your barriers and realize you may be falling into a negative pattern of thinking, the process can be shifted in a positive direction. Here are some methods to help you find your faith:

- Empty yourself of negative thoughts.
  - Be aware of negative thoughts coming to you.
  - Recognize them.
  - Identify them.
  - Let them go!
- Replace these thoughts with positive reminders to yourself that success is coming no matter what.
- Remind yourself that this "detour" is part of the process, and is giving you the tools and the strength needed to progress toward your goal. (It is NOT a reason to give up or feel defeated.)
- Remind yourself in writing. In your journal, keep a list of your intentions (ONLY the POSITIVE reminders of what is coming to you!)
- Read this list often (especially when you've experienced a temporary setback or negative experience.) Read it out loud. Feel the feelings of excitement that each intention will bring you. Read it and feel the positive emotions as if you've already received the items.

"Your living is determined not so much by what life brings you as by the attitude you bring to life; not so much by what happens to you as by the way your mind looks at what happens."

—Kahlil Gibran

Faith allows you to feel happy despite circumstances that may not initially appear to be positive. Faith is believing what you want is already yours. It might take a minute, or it might take years to accomplish. Either way, faith is knowing it IS going to happen, and it will happen in the right time.

Have Faith in The Universe

Remember, nature and the universe are perfect. Choose to have faith in yourself. Have faith in the universe, nature, a higher power, supreme intelligence, or whatever you believe in. No matter what you may face along the path to your destination, unwavering faith makes you untouchable. When you're vibrating in a certain way, whether you're feeling good or feeling bad, the universe is going to correspond to that vibration and send you more people, situations and circumstances to match that vibration.

Remember when I mentioned that I had even been homeless for a time? That's a perfect example of how things will come to you, if you stay positive and have faith. Even though I was sleeping on the street and at times having to ask complete strangers for a quarter or anything they could spare so I could buy food, I never lost my faith in the universe. Soon, I did find a job doing night cleaning at a gym. But the meager paycheck was not enough to cover rent for an apartment. One of the gym staff heard I was looking for a cheap place to stay, and he opened his home to me, gave me a room and said I could pay him later. I will always be grateful for this gesture. Now I had a job, a place to sleep and soon more good things came my way. My boss at the gym, seeing how hard I worked and hearing about my circumstances, generously offered to give me an old car he had, saying I could pay him back when my situation improved. So now I had a job, a place to sleep and the transportation to get to a second job, where I could earn more and I eventually had enough to rent an apartment. So you see, this is how the Law of Attraction works. My positivity brought good things. Don't forget, it's your decision to vibrate positively or negatively. Choose to do it positively, and positive results will follow.

Understanding True Faith

Sometimes people think they have faith, when in reality, they don't. In their

"Our greatest weakness lies in giving up. The most certain way to succeed is always to try just one more time."

—Thomas Edison

thoughts, prayers or mediations they focus on a particular burden (or many burdens) and they ask to please be relieved of the burden because of how much pain, stress or frustration it's causing them. They focus on their burdens and the negative feelings, asking for it to go away.

For example, someone may be struggling with money and financial concerns and says a prayer to please NOT let them experience this lack of money and suffering anymore. They have so many bills and not enough money in the bank to pay them. They don't want to be in debt anymore. They're focused on the pain and suffering of debt and ask for the suffering to be taken away. With this kind of presentation, experiencing positive results is difficult. First, this person is so focused on what he doesn't want, he has no room for thoughts of what he DOES want and how wonderful that would feel. Second, by placing his focus on his suffering and what he wants to go away, he remains in a negative state of vibrational energy. His thoughts are still on his misfortune and the negative feelings it has caused, and so he will continue to attract more situations and circumstances that match the way he is feeling and vibrating. Changing the focus of his thoughts and prayers will easily shift the way this person is vibrating, and it will change the kinds of things he attracts to his life.

Opposites of Faith

Another example of someone's misconception of faith is a person who faithfully prays or meditates and asks for something as a goal. She visualizes it wonderfully, she pictures it, she feels it, and she imagines herself in that achievement for a moment of excitement. As she finishes picturing it, she begins the thought process of, "How in the world am I going to attain that?" And a list of reasons begins to flow as to why it's going to be so difficult, or perhaps even impossible. The downward thought process includes ideas like:

- I don't have enough money.
- What if I'm not smart enough?
- I'm not good-looking enough.
- I don't know how to accomplish this.
- I don't deserve that.
- I don't have enough time to work on it.

- What are other people going to think?
- That is going to be so difficult!
- I never seem to get what I want.

These are the examples of the "opposites of faith." Thinking like this will automatically create a vibration of resistance to your desires, and this vibration will attract negative circumstances, situations and experiences, which will delay your process or even take you in the opposite direction and make your success impossible.

Everything you want and desire is within your grasp. The process is quite simple: First you have to want. Then you have to believe. Then you can receive and achieve. If you look at something as being impossible, for you, it really will be impossible. By focusing on obstacles, you can't truly picture success in your mind, and you create a swirl of negative energy and doubt. You vibrate on that frequency, and you continue to focus on every obstacle or every excuse as to why you can't do it.

Ask and You Will Receive

In many ancient teachings, and particularly in the teachings of Jesus, he said when you ask, it's already yours, and the Father already knows what you want before you even ask. You just have to have faith that you'll receive it, and you WILL receive it. When you have these thoughts and feelings, the universe will correspond to positive vibration and bring everything your way that will make your journey to success possible.

Have faith that all of the people, situations and experiences you need to be successful will be presented to you at the right time on your path to your desires. Stay focused on what you asked for. Have faith and feel good — feel happy it is coming.

Keeping Your Faith

Of course, planning a course of action is necessary, and there are steps and sub-steps you must follow to accomplish your goals. But you must follow your steps with faith and without fear. Maintaining a strong belief throughout your journey will keep you moving forward, despite any unexpected events, and nature in all its wisdom, will provide for you at the right time.

If you wish to grow a peach tree, there are a number of steps you must follow, as well as tools and supplies that are required. Once you plan, prepare and follow the correct steps to plant and nourish the seed, it will grow. Nature takes care of that in the proper time. If you check on it immediately the following day, and you don't see the tree, you wouldn't just walk away discouraged because your tree didn't simply appear with peaches all over it! This is when you need to have your unwavering faith. This is when you know there cannot be any other way. The tree needs time to grow, but it's going to grow. Your peach tree will be there bearing its fruit ... in its destined time.

When you experience challenges or feelings of doubt, impatience or discouragement, that's when you must use the power of positive thinking to shift your thoughts. As we learned earlier, shifting your thoughts will shift your feelings ... which will shift your energy... and ultimately shift your experiences. Your success is already on its way. You just have to be ready to receive it, and have the FAITH to believe it's already yours.

Essential Element #5: *Patience*
My path to becoming a kickboxing world champion was not one I traveled overnight. I had to learn from ancient masters, contemporary success teachers, and my own mistakes and triumphs. But I am able to share all these things with you today because of what I learned on my path to achieving my dream of becoming not only a kickboxing world champion, but a seven-time world champion! The fifth and final essential element for conditioning the mind is patience. Patience was a quality I learned all too well through my own journey. As I look back and contemplated the importance of all five of the essential elements I developed, I realized patience was of vital importance.

Patience goes hand in hand with faith. The element of patience will allow you to endure whatever time it will take and whatever work is required to get where you're going. As I trained physically, mentally and spiritually to become a world champion, there was always a burning desire within me that kept me focused, disciplined and committed. The road was a long one, but I knew I wouldn't stop until I achieved the title. Looking back on each step I took along the way, I see the purpose of each minute, hour, day, month and year it took me to accomplish my dreams. I learned to look for and recognize the tools and strength I gained from each experience, hardship and setback as well as each small triumph. Sometimes, the benefits aren't understood until later, especially the events that initially felt like detours or failures.

Finding Joy in the Process

The art of patience can be difficult to master, especially when we feel so excited about the life we are working toward. Not rushing the perfect timing of the universe, and knowing success will come exactly when it's supposed to, is in itself a challenge. Of course, you always continue to work toward your goal and do what you need to do in order to maintain a forward momentum, but at the same time you must have patience and must develop the ability to be still when action is not required. In addition, if you're working toward mastering all of the five essential elements, you'll come to find joy in the *process* of creating your ideal life. You'll find reasons to be happy and thankful in the moment, NOT just waiting to experience your true happiness only when your goal is reached. Find joy in the present moment. Work on what you need to, but also make sure you do things daily to feel good.

As we've discussed (and I repeat this often because it's so important!), when you already know what you want with certainty, your job is to create a positive vibrational state in tune with your desires, so you can attract the most efficient path to making them a reality. When your energy is in tune with your desires, the essential element of patience enables you to allow the universe time to align itself and present you with everything you need. It may work on a timeline slightly different from yours, so the key is never to doubt success is coming, and patiently move forward with what you need to be doing!

Placing Your Order in the Universe

Imagine you have a catalog from a store you love. You've been browsing through the pages, admiring each and every item, and you've earmarked the pages of the items you just can't do without. Let's say it's Friday afternoon, around 4:00 p.m. You've decided that today is the day and now is the time to place your order! You grab your credit card, pick up the phone, and carefully order each item, giving the telephone agent each item number. You happily complete your order at approximately 4:05 p.m. and hang up the phone, excited that your items will be delivered to your house sometime soon. You know it's coming, and you're excited!

Now, let's say at 4:15 p.m. — just ten minutes later — you're wondering where your stuff is. You impatiently look at your watch, pace around your house, look out the window, and you get worried the items may not even be coming. You call the store to complain because you haven't received your products yet and you ask the representative if she's absolutely sure they really will be sent. This sounds pretty silly, right? However, it illustrates the point of how we often decide what we want, we are excited about it at first, then for a variety of reasons we get impatient and we start to doubt and wonder if what we have asked for will even materialize.

In our example, when your catalog order was placed, it would require some time for the person who received it to send it to the warehouse to be filled. Time is needed to access the product, process the record, pack it, wrap it and mail it or put it on a truck for delivery. Always remember, once you "place your order," your job is to just feel excitement that your order is on its way! You don't have to doubt it or wonder about it. It's ordered and paid for! Have patience knowing it will get to you just as soon as possible — in the time it takes for the particular order to be processed. Some orders can be filled more quickly than others. But once you place the order, just relax and know it will arrive.

Be Joyful While You Wait

I mentioned before that sometimes we need to sit back and be still when action is not required. However, how do we know when action is NOT required? This may be difficult to determine, especially when we want so badly to achieve something and we are working extremely hard to make it happen. In working so hard, sometimes we turn it into a tedious, painful process. There was a time when people believed that unless the process was difficult and painful, the reward was undeserved. You know — no pain, no gain.

"There is nothing that wastes the body like worry, and who has any faith in God should be ashamed to worry about anything whatsoever."

—Gandhi

"Working" toward something wonderful and joyful should feel wonderful and joyful. The most efficient path toward your goal shouldn't be painful and tedious. Yes, there will be times when hard work and self-discipline are required, but the focus on the joy of what you're working toward should allow you to keep a positive frame of mind throughout the journey. Otherwise, it may not be the right path or the most efficient path for you.

When you're vibrating in tune with your desires and the universe, sometimes NO work is required, and we need to simply sit back, observe and watch for the path to be shown to us. We don't have to worry and think about which path to take. We just know the next step on our path toward our destination will be illuminated when it is the right time. This "illumination" may take the form of meeting in exactly the right moment the right person who will help advance you toward your goal. It may be a circumstance presented to you that just feels so right, there is absolutely no question in your mind it's the right choice. As long as you're vibrating positively, your process shouldn't involve tedious work that makes you feel miserable. The correct path will FEEL right.

Big Orders Don't Take Longer

It doesn't matter how big or small your goals are. Those measurements of magnitude live only in our minds, when actually in terms of delivery by the universe, it doesn't matter. We often think if a goal is bigger, it must be more difficult to acquire. However, in order for ANYTHING to materialize in our lives, big or small, it will be born in the same way — as a result of our thoughts and corresponding vibrational state. Our job is to formulate a clear picture of what we want, and then do whatever we need to do to maintain a positive vibrational energy. And when we face detours, delays or roadblocks, we must remind ourselves we are gaining tools and strength. Seek and find the seeds of benefit, then just relax and have patience.

The Limitations of Logic

As humans, our minds are always active. We are always looking for solutions to problems, and searching for logical answers to questions. In our rush to achieve success as quickly as possible, we forget about patience and forget we shouldn't be forcing things to happen before its time. Sometimes we seek answers that lead us in the right direction, but other times the harder we try to seek logical answers, the more difficult it becomes to find them, and we end up losing our good judgment. We are cerebrally looking for answers, and trying to almost scientifically decide where we need to proceed next on our path. In those moments, we may be motivated by frustration, desperation, impatience or other negative emotions, and we can't make decisions wisely. Most people use logic and conscious reasoning to find answers, when there are times when it may be better to find the answers in another way. Logic has many limitations — it's limited to the information provided by the senses, and sometimes the knowledge we need is found beyond the senses.

> **"I hear and I forget ... I see and I
> remember ... I do and I understand."**
>
> **—Ancient Chinese Proverb**

As part of the process in developing the essential element of patience in *The Master Method*, we must gain a little understanding of *knowledge*, and the three ways in which we acquire knowledge.

The Acquisition of Knowledge

There are three types of knowledge we acquire in a variety of ways:

- Knowledge through senses
- Knowledge through experience
- Knowledge through intuition

The first type is the knowledge we gain through our **senses**. This is the knowledge we are able to process from what we see, hear, touch and taste. All of this knowledge gives us information we process in our brains, in order to understand the matter in front of us.

The second kind of knowledge is the most powerful and the longest lasting — the knowledge we gain through **experience**. By *experiencing*, we learn and gain knowledge we will not forget because it is stored in our memories of experiences and in our subconscious minds. Although we may not consciously remember an experience, our subconscious mind never forgets.

The third type of knowledge is gained through **intuition**. This is the knowledge gained through our "extra" sense and it guides us through our lives. Intuition takes us beyond what we can see and beyond our logical thought. We can't confirm or see the answer; we just know. Intuition is the feeling inside ... the feeling you get without logic or judgment. Sometimes all logical evidence points you in one direction, but your intuition takes you in another.

Trust Your Intuition
When you let your *mind* work with your intuition, it's not your intuition working anymore, but your brain ... your logic.

Intuition is the most powerful of all knowledge. It's not based on the senses, but on the true essence of the matter, which is not always understandable by the brain or logical thought. Intuition has no limitations with time, and it's connected to a higher plane of existence. Your intuition is in direct connection with the universe, nature or supreme power or supreme intelligence. When you truly learn to use your intuition, an incredible universal source of knowledge is available to you for guidance.

If you're faced with a decision at a crossroads, let your intuition tell you which way is the right way. One way will always instinctively feel better than the other. As long as you're truly using your intuition and not your logical thought, you'll know which path to take. It may even turn out to be a path you least expected, but if you truly trust your intuition in making your decision, it will prove to be the path that was meant to lead you to your destination.

If you were to test the accuracy of your true intuition, you would be amazed to realize, without logic of the mind clouding a decision, the right answer is always simple. As long as you put aside any logical thoughts and preconceived ideas of what you THINK is the right thing to do, you can learn to discover and feel the incredible power of your intuition.

If you reach a point where you're not sure of the next step to take, don't try to rush the answer. Rushing to move forward and desperately seeking the answer will not make it suddenly appear. Sometimes all you need to do is wait ... patiently. Sit back, relax and watch, almost like watching a movie... and see how the next step naturally unfolds in front of you. When the time is right, and when you're ready to receive it, the next step will be shown to you. Always keep your end result in mind, be happy you're on your way to receiving it, and have faith and patience that the best path will be presented to you exactly when it should be.

EXERCISE: DON'T SWEAT THE SMALL STUFF

The exercise of patience can be extremely difficult. The mind is always in a hurry wanting things done right away or wanting answers immediately, even if we are not ready to receive them. We always want to force nature to give us what we want when we want it, and we often forget nature's timing is perfect.

One way to exercise patience is to practice with little things. For example, waiting in line at the grocery store, or stopping at a red light are perfect opportunities to practice the art of patience. Allowing yourself to feel irritated or desperate in these situations never helps things move faster. In fact, by giving in to the negative emotions, you're setting yourself up to attract more circumstances that will frustrate you and delay you. Then you find yourself in a negative state of affairs that continues to create negative emotions within you. Make a conscious decision to shift your energy.

Practice keeping your thoughts and emotions positive in every matter, large and small, throughout your day — especially in situations when you need to wait or when you're in a hurry to get somewhere. When you feel negative emotions surfacing, take a few deep breaths ... relax your mind, think of something that makes you feel good and focus your attention on shifting your thoughts and emotions positively. Let go of your tension. Choose to feel good in those moments.

It's time to add a new list to your journal — a list of little exercises you plan on using to develop your patience. Write this patience exercise list and refer to it regularly to remind yourself of things you can do, especially at times when you're feeling impatient.

Remember — choose to enjoy every moment of your life and feel good.

"There is no logical way to the discovery of these elemental laws. There is only the way of intuition, which is helped by a feeling for the order lying behind the appearance."

—Albert Einstein

Step 3: Plan

Planning for Success

You're well on your way to a wonderful life, now that you've chosen your destination (Step 1: Decide) and you're actively and consciously working on achieving your most healthy, positive frame of mind possible (Step 2: Condition) for the journey and beyond. Now you're ready to actually lay out a plan that will enable you to materialize your desires.

This is Step 3 in *The Master Method*. Now the excitement REALLY begins! You have your goal already in your mind. You've written it down. You've read it. You've re-read it. You've pictured it and visualized it in every way. Now let's move forward toward your destination by creating a PLAN.

Make a Plan and Commit to It

When I was a teenager, I got up very early and I did 180 pushups, 180 situps, 180 squats and 1,000 kicks faithfully every day before school. I never missed a day. A few years ago, I ran into someone I had dated in my early days of training. We were talking about those times and she reminded me that I always kept her waiting before we went out. I had a set workout that was part of my plan to become world champion and nothing — not even a date with a beautiful girl — could keep me from my training. If I set 180 pushups as my goal, then I did 180 pushups, not

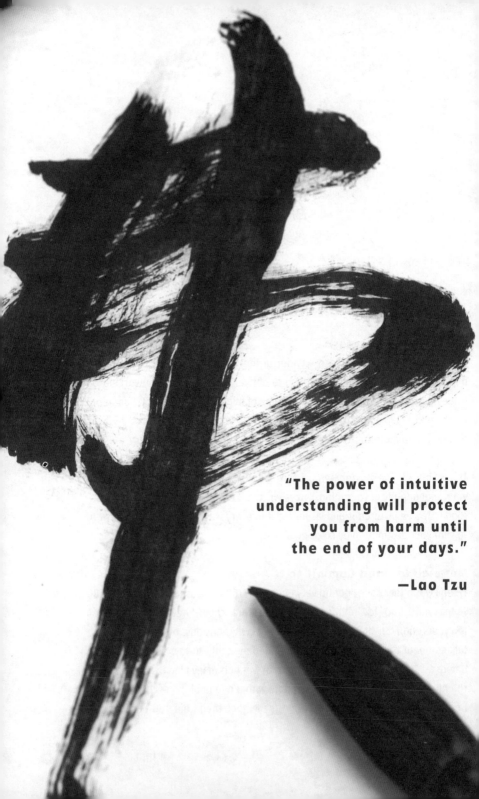

"The power of intuitive understanding will protect you from harm until the end of your days."

—Lao Tzu

100 ... or 150 ... or even 179! I had my plan and I stuck to it, no matter what.

Charting Your Route

Once you know without a doubt what your destination is AND you're working on conditioning your mind to keep you in the strongest most positive mindset possible, you'll need a roadmap to get you to your dreams. So begin by outlining your plan. Otherwise, you could end up wasting time and energy going down paths that will only delay your success. Your roadmap will allow you to take the most efficient and timely route to your end point. Once you've mapped out your plan, your positive thoughts, feelings and energy will work most efficiently in creating opportunities and experiences that will enable you to achieve your success.

Why Make a Plan?

Imagine you lived in Buffalo, New York, and you decide to take a road trip to Los Angeles, California. You're excited about going to LA, anticipating the smell of the ocean and the 80-degree warmth, and you're looking forward to being on the West Coast very soon. You could just hop in your car with no compass or map, guess which way is west and start driving. At each crossroad, you'd have to presume which direction to turn, perhaps to discover it's wrong and you need to make a U-turn. You're not sure where you are or how to get where you're going. Soon you feel as though you've gotten nowhere.

Taking a trip this way would create endless frustration (not to mention waste a lot of gas), and because you have no direction and have been driving around in circles making no progress, you may even give up and decide not to make the trip at all. You knew where you wanted to go, but you had no plan of *how* to get there.

On the other hand, carefully planning your route and having a map before you begin your journey would make this trip much more enjoyable. And you'd arrive at your destination more quickly. You wouldn't be worried along the way, since you planned it ahead of time, and you could even enjoy the scenery, feeling relaxed and looking forward to your arrival. Even if you run into unexpected roadblocks, detours, traffic or bad weather that weren't part of the original plan ... as long as you keep your destination in mind ... AND your plan allows for minor

"Create a definite plan for carrying out your desire and begin at once, whether you are ready or not, to put this plan into action."

—Napoleon Hill

detours, you can make adjustments. In the end, you might even find yourself on a better road.

Build in Flexibility

The purpose of developing your roadmap is to determine specifically what you need to do to accomplish your goal. These are the exact steps you'll take to get to your final destination. Even though you're creating a detailed plan, always allow for unexpected challenges and detours, and be prepared to revise steps as necessary. As long as you maintain the faith that challenges are meant to provide you with the tools you need to keep moving forward, you WILL continue to move forward! Plan well, but always be flexible.

Once you've outlined your plan, remember it's not definite, rigid or set in stone. It's meant to be a simple, MODIFIABLE guideline to help you take action and enable you to go after your goal one piece at a time. You must be able to adjust your plan and adapt it when you realize one of the steps may not be working, or if it's taking you in a wrong direction.

If you reach a point where you're not sure about how to adjust your plan or which path to take, don't panic. Just take a deep breath, pause, watch and listen. Trust your intuition and have faith the answers will come. Try to be receptive and open to the answers whenever and however they are shown to you. Don't be concerned about when and how it will happen. Just have faith in the right path being presented to you when you're ready to receive it.

If things don't feel right, trust the feeling. Then be receptive to the other opportunities that are waiting for you to notice them. The right path will FEEL right. Sit back and relax for a moment, or perhaps for a few days or even a few weeks. Observe the opportunities, people and situations around you. Be patient, and have unwavering faith that the right path will be shown to you. And when it's shown to you — TAKE ACTION!

Bumps in the Road Make You Stronger

On your journey to success, please remember that the people and experiences you encounter along the way are vital to giving you the tools, strength and character to complete the rest of your journey. No experience or encounter is an accident or a waste of time. You'll always benefit somehow from each person you meet and from each experience, even if it initially feels like a tough challenge.

For example, trying people and problematic experiences teach us patience, compassion and perseverance. Accept every individual and experience you encounter with gratitude, because you're becoming a stronger, wiser, more patient person as a result. These experiences are preparing you for the next step in achieving your goal. Don't be discouraged. Move forward through the difficulties, over the bumps in the road and around the roadblocks, because once you come out on the other side, you'll understand how much stronger you are. You'll find yourself even closer to the life of your dreams, as long as you continue to vibrate positively.

Visual Reminders

You already know what you want, and you've written it down. Now, write it again! Write it on a piece of paper and tape it to your mirror. Put another one in your wallet, on your desk and in your car. In fact, write it down right now!

The more you remind yourself of your destination, the more you'll keep yourself in the right frame of mind.

One Step at a Time

Now, you must make it clear in your mind what exact steps are necessary to get you to where you're going. Start by writing down a general outline of incremental steps to your goal. Gradually make each step more specific until you have a very clear detailed strategy. Every step can be defined as a small goal in itself, leading you to your big goal. And be sure to celebrate the accomplishment of each one!

Each incremental step allows you to focus in the short term on one small goal.

Sometimes if a goal is too large, it seems unattainable because it feels so far away. You may find yourself getting lost in the process. You get discouraged or impatient and you may even give up because the big goal seems so far off. However, if you divide the large goal into smaller sub-goals you can complete them one by one and eventually reach the large goal in a much more efficient manner.

In order to achieve a black belt in martial arts, for example, the first step is to learn the most basic techniques in order to earn your first belt. After earning that belt, the focus is shifted toward the next set of techniques to earn the next belt. Each belt level consists of its own list of requirements that must be met in order to achieve that belt. Each belt is celebrated as its own accomplishment, but all the while, the student is keeping the final goal in mind — the black belt.

Similarly, if you wish to become a doctor, there are specific steps, such as pre-med classes, the MCAT exam and gaining a certain amount of practical experience in order to be accepted to medical school, and each of these steps is a small goal in itself. Once in medical school, each class may also be considered a small sub-goal toward your ultimate goal of becoming a physician. You take each step incrementally, earning your small achievements, but always keeping in mind and visualizing what you're ultimately working toward. You actually SEE yourself achieving it and you feel the excitement NOW.

Little Steps Add Up to Big Accomplishments

No matter what you hope to achieve — losing weight, earning a certain amount of money or improving a relationship — outlining your plan to reach your goal is vital to getting there most efficiently. Breaking your large goal down into smaller goals allows for the achievement of small victories that will make you feel successful along the way. These victories will motivate you to work even harder and more enthusiastically toward the next step. Eventually, each step will be accomplished, and your final destination will be reached!

Always keep your main goal in mind, even while you're taking the little steps and celebrating your incremental achievements. Never lose sight of the final destination. Don't get so immersed in the smaller steps that you forget the ultimate goal. It's far too easy to get stuck in the process, stop moving forward and never reach your endpoint. You may get too comfortable where you are and lose your drive. Avoid the possibility by reminding yourself often of the wonderful end result.

Keep Your Eyes on the Prize

Keeping your final goal in mind is also vital in overcoming unexpected circumstances that may frustrate you or challenge your motivation to keep going. Sometimes the "clutter" from the past we spoke of earlier begins to accumulate in our minds again, especially if we are faced with challenges. We allow fear or unworthiness or doubt to affect our thoughts and actions, or we reach a point where we don't want to leave our comfort zone physically, mentally or emotionally. It's at these moments when you must really rely on your faith in the universe and remember, your path WILL take you where you want to go. You'll reach your destination, as long as you stay positive and feel good.

Keep your feelings positive and generate good feelings by visualizing your goals often. Immerse yourself in activities and around people who make you feel good and share your positive energy. Go back to the Feel Good list you made in Step 1 of *The Master Method* and use it to regenerate your positive mindset. Read books that make you feel good. Watch programs that make you happy. Exercise and stay active so your body feels healthy. Surround yourself with what makes you feel peaceful and happy, because all of these good feelings will create incredibly powerful energy to keep you on track. Here's a reminder of some great feel good fixers:

- Go for a walk
- Meditate
- Spend time with positive people who make you feel happy
- Watch a funny movie
- Play your favorite sport
- Listen to music that lifts your spirits
- Experience the sights and sounds of nature
- Spend time with a beloved pet
- Go to the bookstore and browse through the feel good books and music
- Have a favorite delicious (and healthy) meal
- READ THIS BOOK AGAIN!
- Do what makes you smile, laugh and feel joyful
- Do what brings you peace

Put Your Plan Into Gear

Now that you've learned how to map out your plan, it's time to take action! Get started right away, while everything is fresh in your memory, by using this next exercise to get your ideas out of your mind and onto paper. Once you begin, you'll see how simple it is to focus on one small step at a time. So "stay in the car" no matter what twists and turns may lie ahead, keep driving forward, and before you know it, you'll arrive at the destination of your dreams.

EXERCISE: CHECKLIST OF STEPS

In your journal, write down at least five steps necessary for the attainment of your goals in each of the five areas of life: Career, Finances, Relationships, Health and Inner Peace. Give yourself a timeline for each step and indicate it clearly.

Now make daily checklists of things to accomplish toward those steps, and with each task you check off, allow yourself to feel a sense of advancement and satisfaction that you're moving closer and closer to your ultimate goal.

Keep in mind, you may modify steps along the way. If something isn't working, revise your plan accordingly. Plan well, but allow for flexibility.

Career		Finances		Relationships		Health		Inner Peace	
Step	Date	Step	Date	Step	Date	Step	Date	Step	Date

Step 4: Create!

Congratulations! You've now reached the last step in *The Master Method* for building a life of happiness, success and inner peace. You should be very proud of yourself for the exercises and work you've already begun.

Let's quickly review the DCPC Formula:

Step 1: Decide

You began by deciding what you want. You started a journal, where you acknowledged what you don't want and listed what you do want. You assessed your starting point and learned about the power of thought and the thought-feelings-energy connection. I talked about choosing the positive path and you began thinking about your goals in the five areas of life: Career, Finances, Relationships, Health and Inner Peace. Here you learned that you are the creator of your own reality.

Step 2: Condition

In this chapter, I introduced the concept of conditioning your mind for success through five essential elements: Gratitude, Humility, Positivity, Faith and Patience. You discovered you can change your thinking, that losing is nothing more than a part of winning, and that it's possible to reset your default for positivity. I also gave you some techniques for overcoming roadblocks and dealing with difficult people, as well as sustaining your faith and practicing patience.

Step 3: Plan

Now we got down to the importance of preparing a roadmap and sticking to it. I showed you how to get to your large goals faster by creating smaller incremental goals and building flexibility into your plan.

Step 4: Create!

So here we are, near the end of your introduction to *The Master Method* and the beginning of your exciting journey to success in all aspects of your life. In this final step we'll discuss some vital elements for staying on track and achieving your goals: self-discipline, enthusiasm, how to break through barriers and how to stay positive. Then I'll give you a few last motivational tips and some final exercises.

Self-Discipline and Strength of Mind

When I decided at the age of 15 to become a kickboxing world champion, I knew it wasn't going to happen overnight. I knew it would require a huge amount of conditioning and the development of techniques. I knew I also needed experience to understand the mechanics of fighting, and the work required would be extremely difficult. BUT I also knew, without a doubt, where I wanted to be, and I knew I would do whatever it took.

In order to fight at a world championship level, a large part of my plan was not just to get into shape, but also to work until I had the best-conditioned lightweight class body in the world. In order to do that, I had to get up early EVERY SINGLE DAY and do the work required to carry out my plan. It takes self-discipline. But how exactly do you develop the discipline you need once you've started work on your plan?

Self-Discipline Is a Process in Itself

Self-discipline is the process of being able to control your thoughts and actions. It's the process of doing what you're supposed to do every day, in order to carry out the instructions you've given yourself for the attainment of your goal. It's being able to do what you must do, regardless of your state of mind — even if you're tired, and even if you don't feel like it.

It Starts with Desire

You must have a burning desire — a desire that fills you with so much excitement, anticipation and pleasure you feel as though it will overflow. This goes back to our discussion of keeping your eyes on the prize — your ultimate goal. While carrying out your instructions for the day, your frame of mind will dictate whether it will be a pleasant or an unpleasant experience. Don't forget, it's your choice as to what frame of mind you sustain throughout your day. If your mind is focused on being tired or being displeased, the completion of any task will be much more difficult, and it will take even more effort to complete it. If you wake up in the morning, complaining about all the things on your list, unhappily drag yourself out of bed, dreading the day ahead, you'll more than likely find more and more to complain about throughout your day, and everything you try to accomplish will end up feeling like an unpleasant chore. On the other hand, if you wake up and look forward to the things you'll accomplish, you'll choose to feel happy about your day. As a result, more good things will be presented to you, and it will be easier to complete your tasks.

The Every Day Rule

Every day is important, and each day you should actively do something — big or small — to bring you closer to your goal. Look at each task as a section of your goal, and the completion of each task as the achievement of part of the big goal. Whatever task is appointed for the day must be completed THAT DAY. Carry out your own instructions with no excuses. Don't waste a moment. Be proactive and take the initiative every single day. This active state of being will keep you vibrating positively. And understand that the quality, speed and amount of success you'll receive are also directly related to our next discussion point: enthusiasm.

The Importance of Enthusiasm

The great success teacher, Napoleon Hill said, "There are no short cuts to great achievements." You must do the work, and you have to do it well ... every last bit of

"However many holy words you read, however many you speak, what good would it do if you don't act upon them."

—Buddha

it. Your success depends not only on doing what you must, but also on *the way* you perform your tasks. If you work without feeling good about it, the results will reflect that. Or, worse yet, you might not see results at all. So you also need the self-discipline to do the work to the VERY BEST of your ability. Carry out your plan with enthusiasm!

For many years, my training routine in preparation for competitions was to start each day, with 45 minutes of running. This was only a fraction of my training and it was just the beginning of my morning. Following my 45-minute run (which also included sprinting and jumping) I would head to the boxing gym for 3 hours to work my hands on the speed bag, heavy bag and pads, also work on reaction time drills and sparring. From the boxing gym, it was time to teach martial arts classes at karate school until 9 p.m., after which I would begin the third section of my training in the late evening. For 2 hours, I worked on kicking and leg conditioning with kicking pads, sparring with my feet, speed drills and endurance drills. I finished my training about 11:00 p.m., and by the time I got home I was absolutely exhausted and often times beat up. But I knew this work was necessary because I wanted to become the best!

The next morning, the routine started all over again. Now, to get up and follow this training program for a day or two is one thing. However, to carry out these instructions every single day for months and months is completely different. Often, I was so physically spent, with aching muscles and, on occasion, injuries. I would look ahead, see the day in front of me just the same as the day before and the day before. Regardless of the schedule, regardless of the weather, and regardless of the pain I was feeling, I still had to get up every morning to train ... and sometimes my mind and body made it unbelievably difficult.

It's All about Attitude
What I learned throughout those years is that it was my CHOICE to get up and either hate what I was doing, or do it knowing this was getting me closer to becoming a world champion. As I lie there early in the morning, I would consciously remind myself what I wanted to accomplish, and I would visualize the end result. Feeling the joy, hearing the cheers from the crowd, feeling the rush of happiness and pride at the moment of reaching my destination.

I would also remind myself of how grateful I was for my health, family and friends and I would actively bring myself into a positive mindset. I was able to consciously and intentionally feel good about what I needed to accomplish that day, and so I would get up, and literally say to myself out loud, "It's going to be a GREAT DAY." I thought about how much I was going to improve and I KNEW the world championship was already on its way, and I felt excited. This excitement gave me the energy to not only get up, but to get up with enthusiasm and attack my tasks.

I felt happy to be improving, regardless if it was 17 degrees or if there was snow and ice on the ground. I was happy to be that much closer to my goal and this positive mental attitude took me down the path to become a world champion, not only once but seven times.

Breaking the Barriers

Sometimes your unconditioned mind will take over and try and trick you into doing things the easy way, such as putting things off until tomorrow or telling you, "I know you're tired. You should just rest today and then do better tomorrow." Or your mind may even try and tell you, "This isn't worth the effort. Maybe you should just stop now. Just give up. Then you can relax!"

Negative thoughts create barriers that may stem from some of the deep-seeded feelings we talked about earlier. Regardless of where these feelings originate, it is only you that allow them to hinder your path to success. You must make a conscious decision to plow through these barriers. Easier said than done? No. You can do it! Use these pointers when you need help:

- Recognize these feelings when they appear
- Identify those feelings (doubt, worry, fear, unworthiness)
- Turn those negative feelings around by focusing on feeling good
- DO things that make you feel good
- Remind yourself that you ARE worthy, you don't need to fear and you are capable
- As long as you're moving forward with joy and enthusiasm, doing your best and feeling good, you won't fail

- Choose to not allow others to disrupt the strong positive feelings you've worked so hard to attain

These things will give you the fuel to do what you need to do in the very best way you can — with enthusiasm. If you're genuine in your enthusiasm, the people around you will also feel it. With every interaction, make others feel your enthusiasm. If you create and maintain positive energy around you, this will create more positive energy that will surround the people you encounter.

Shifting from Negative to Positive

Monitoring thoughts and shifting them to maintain a positive frame of mind is one of the most difficult things for any human being to master. Sometimes it seems impossible to find that positive seed, especially when everything feels like it's going wrong around you. You're overwhelmed, frustrated, discouraged and you feel as though you're failing. This is when you need to stop. Give yourself a break.

You're certainly not alone in experiencing these feelings. You are human! Maybe you're tired. Allow yourself rest. Take some time to back away from the frustration and the discouragement and just let yourself breathe very peacefully for a moment. Close your eyes, and breathe very slowly in through your nose, and out through your mouth. Consciously relax each muscle in your body from the top of your head down to the tips of your toes. Feel yourself becoming more and more relaxed. Allow yourself this moment, and imagine all of the frustration leaving and being replaced with peace and calm. Enjoy this feeling and sit with it for a little while.

Once you've restored a sense of peace and calm within you, now restore that picture in your mind of what you want. Don't think about your day or your frustrations, but think of your destination. Picture it, and enjoy it and shift your feelings back to a positive vibrational state.

Helpful thoughts for shifting gears:
- This experience is strengthening me
- This experience is providing me with valuable tools I will need later
- This experience is giving me wisdom I will need

- This experience is showing me the contrast, so I will really appreciate the joy of overcoming this obstacle
- This experience is temporary
- The faster I can shift my energy back to positive, the faster I will be back on the right path to my goal

An Honest Look Inside

One of the conversations I had with one of my wisest teachers, the Tibetan Lama Tinku Nyima Rinpoche, was a life-changing moment for me. One evening as I visited him in his private chamber, he was explaining to me the importance of self-discipline in order to carry one's life in a positive way, and avoiding negative thoughts and negative actions. As I listened to these teachings, overwhelming feelings of repentance washed over me and I felt dreadful as images of things I had done in my past came to my mind. I told him of these feelings I was experiencing at that moment. He simply smiled, and he said, "Good." Puzzled, I asked my teacher, "Why do you refer to these feelings I'm having as 'good'?" He smiled again and gently explained, "Because now, you know what you don't want to be."

To remain positive, you must first understand the root of your thoughts and determine where they truly originate. Don't waste your energy or use it up on negative emotions such as anger, jealousy or hate. For example, if you're angry, understand that being angry isn't going to solve your problem. It would be much better to use that energy to find a positive solution.

Don't look for excuses or blame other people or circumstances for your negative state of mind. We are 100% responsible for our emotions and for truly understanding why we feel jealous, angry or any other negative emotion. No one else causes us to feel these feelings. Learn to be honest with yourself and develop the self-discipline to understand why you feel as you do. When you're going down a negative path of thoughts and feelings, consciously take yourself through a thought process of questions.

Ask yourself:

- What am I feeling right now?
- Why do I feel this way?
- Is it helping me?
- How can I handle this in a positive way?

Don't Let Your Ego Take Control

Your ego will find any excuse to justify and place blame on others for your negative thoughts, feelings and actions ("I am really angry because of HIS behavior," or "I'm not going to help her because she was rude."). Learn to become the master of your own thoughts and emotions. YOU control your emotions and what you allow yourself to feel about a person or a situation. Once you can truly understand the nature of your thought and are able to master controlling your vibrational energy, you become invincible — the master of your mind. Understanding your thoughts will improve your relationships with everyone you encounter.

EXERCISE: REVIEW THE DAY

Every day, try to find a quiet moment. Close your eyes. Relax your body. Visualize your muscles beginning to relax. When you introduce yourself to the relaxation state, let thoughts come into your mind. Don't repress them. Let them come, then let them go. Let them in, then let them out.

Now rerun your day, beginning with the last encounter with the last person in your day. What did you do? What did you say? What was the interaction? Don't identify yourself with the situation. If it was happy, don't get happy. If it was sad, don't get sad. If something made you angry, look at the situation but don't get angry. Just look at it ... and let it out. Watch it like a movie. Move on to the situation before that, and the one before that, and the one before that, until you see yourself waking up that morning.

You've now gone through the whole day of experiences and you've replayed everything you encountered — without the emotion. You're now able to have a different view of your day, and this allows you to remove any negativity that may have resulted from your experiences. You've shifted yourself to a positive frame of mind, which will keep you on the right path of doing what you need to do — completing your tasks and carrying out your plan for success.

A Few Last Motivational Tips

1 — You are worthy of success.

Don't let the voices of your past tell you you won't succeed. Free your mind from those voices. You were created to mirror perfection—that's the true essence of who you are. Your only job is to go back and reconnect with that source of perfection, with that infinite intelligence who created you. The wonderful life you truly desire is yours! You must really believe you deserve it. The moment you do that, you open the gates for a successful life filled with abundance. You are a magnificent being, but a magnificent life will only manifest when you decide to acknowledge that YOU ARE WORTHY, YOU ARE CAPABLE, and YOU TRULY DESERVE the life you desire.

2 — Because you're connected to infinite intelligence, your power is unlimited.

Nature and the universe are perfection. Don't feel powerless and become a victim of circumstances. You have the POWER to CREATE the life you truly want. That universal force that drives everything and everyone — the source, infinite intelligence, supreme power, or however you choose to accept it — is present in everyone and everything. When you remain conscious of your connection to this force, your power to create is unlimited!

3 — Don't let fear rule your life.

Fear is one of the main causes of negative thinking and failure, and there are many types of fears that can influence our minds — fear of rejection, fear of failure, fear of embarrassment, fear of poverty, fear of losing the ones you love, fear of "what are they going to say," fear of sickness, fear of death. No matter what kind of fear lives within you, it only holds you back and prevents the expansion of your mind, body and your spirit.

Eradicate your fears. For any fear you may experience, empower yourself with positive affirmations and a plan to walk through your fear, pass it by and leave it behind you. Tell yourself, "If my friends reject me, I'll find new friends who will support me. If I fail, I'll learn a valuable lesson that will help me get closer to my goal. It doesn't matter what others think about me. Their opinions will not diminish what I think of myself or change my focus. If someone I love decides to walk on a different path, my thoughts will be with him, and I will wish him a safe and successful journey. Knowing we are energy beings, death is only a change of state, so I can never be afraid of death." Once again, as long as you focus on what you want, everything you experience will bring you closer to your goal.

4 — Fill yourself with love and compassion.
Love is the most powerful of all emotions. Love will allow you to see the most beautiful colors, and the most beautiful shapes. It will help you see the best in everyone. Love allows you to bypass external layers of personality and find the connection between all beings. Allow yourself to experience this beautiful emotion.

Compassion is the antidote for anger and many other negative emotions. We can feel compassion if we try to understand others and look beyond negative behavior and attempt to understand where the root of their negativity is coming from. It could be a lack of knowledge or their own fears or insecurities.

5 — Find joy in everything that surrounds you.
We are not just in this universe, but we are a part of it. Feel the wind. Listen to the birds. Feel the energy of the trees and the plants. Just enjoy being in the presence of what surrounds you. This awareness and appreciation will bring you a great sense of peace and tranquility. Always give yourself a little time to really acknowledge, appreciate and enjoy your surroundings.

6 — Surround yourself with people who will support your frame of mind, and avoid people who are a negative influence.

"Enthusiasm is the yeast that makes your hopes shine to the stars. Enthusiasm is the sparkle in your eyes, the swing in your gait, the grip of your hand, the irresistible surge of will and energy to execute your ideas."

—Henry Ford

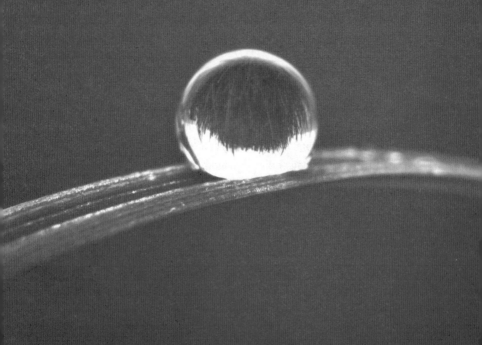

Successful people surround themselves with other successful people. They feed off of each other's positive energy, empowering themselves through their interactions with one another. Their positive energies, knowledge and enthusiasm are wonderful things to share. In contrast, the doom and gloom of surrounding yourself with pessimistic people will have that kind of impact on you as well. Avoid as much as possible interactions with people who criticize or unintentionally put you down, thinking they're giving you their opinion to "help" you. Instead, share your ideas and surround yourself with people who support your frame of mind, or with people from whom you can take proper constructive advice.

7 — Rest well, and create healthy habits.
Taking care of your body and the creation of healthy habits are essential to increase your overall productivity. Having enough rest will increase your level of energy and you'll perform better, and have a better mental attitude. Similarly, proper nutrition will increase the level and quality of your productivity, and it will create an overall wellness within you that will allow you to vibrate positively. Excesses will always have a negative impact on your body, and therefore it will have an impact in the way you perform. Live a life of balance and enjoy the results!

8 — Relax.
Worrying is not going to make what you want come any faster. One of the things many people "like" to do, when they encounter a challenge, is to get extra worried about it. Getting into a worrying frenzy is not going to help you find a solution faster. So change the cycle, change your vibration, focus on what you really want, and you'll begin to attract good things.

9 — Allow time to learn something new.
Always keep your mind open to knowledge. Learn by observing others, by observing nature and everything surrounding you. Learn from a book, from an audio source or from a video. Learn from a teacher, and from each day you live. By constantly expanding your mind, you keep it conditioned to seek and accept knowledge. You will become more equipped to live better and to gain a deeper understanding of life. You'll also gain understanding of yourself and your own nature.

"To enjoy good health, to bring true happiness to one's family, to bring peace to all, one must first discipline and control one's own mind. If a man can control his mind, he can find a way to enlightenment, and all wisdom and virtue will naturally come to him."

—Buddha

10 – Visit a new place.

Once in a while it feels really good to visit a new place. It doesn't have to be a faraway place; it can be somewhere nearby. It doesn't have to require much time. Eat at a new restaurant. Watch a new movie. Go for a walk. I am always trying to find new places to go. I love the mountains or lakes, and when I don't have much time, I try to find a fun place to go with my family, even if it's just a short nature walk somewhere. This helps to renew your energies and it will get you out of a routine you may be falling into. Sometimes people go about their days, day after day on autopilot, doing what they're supposed to do, without any energy or enthusiasm. Experiencing new places, or breaking your routine once in a while, will help you stay excited and enthusiastic! It will refresh your spirit, and it's FUN!

11 – Repeat the following statement out loud each day, and as often as possible.

- I am the creator of my life
- I am in control of my thoughts and my emotions
- I have unlimited power to create the life I desire
- I am so grateful for everything I have
- With every breath I take, inner peace and happiness fills me

12– Take Action

When you have detailed your plan, don't wait! TAKE ACTION. Procrastination will kill any plan in no time. You must be PROACTIVE, so START NOW! Put your plan into practice, even if is not perfect or exactly how you want it to be yet. Anything you haven't figured out yet, the "doing" will quickly teach you and reveal to you what needs to be adjusted in your original plan. Just get started!

Dream Big!

I hope *The Master Method* has inspired you and given you the tools and the confidence to find and follow your innermost dreams. Using the steps, concepts, exercises and visualizations of *The Master Method*, you can finally take control of your life. I've not only shared with you the basics of conditioning yourself for your journey to success, but also the tools you'll need to maintain the right frame of mind for lifelong enjoyment of your accomplishments and continued success in all future pursuits.

Enjoy your life of true happiness. Find the joy in each hour of every day. Appreciate the abundance in your life. Feel your powerful connection to the universe. And feel true peace beginning to take over your entire being. Everything you dream of is possible if you follow each of the steps humbly and conscientiously. Keep moving forward and never give up. Feel good in the process and ENJOY the journey!

I wish you endless successes and peace.

— Master Marco Sies

Learn More about The Master Method

In addition to the material found in this book, you can find excellent supplemental readings, meditations and exercises on *The Master Method* website:

www.themastermethod.com

There you'll find free exercises designed to help you succeed in your daily visualizations, as well as meditations and instructional materials that will guide you step by step on how to relax your mind and create vivid and effective visualizations for the attainment of your goals.

ABOUT THE AUTHOR

Master Marco Sies is a 7-time professional kickboxing world champion, 7th-degree black belt martial arts grandmaster, 2-time Hall of Fame inductee, and a 2008 Master Instructor of the Year awarded at Madison Square Garden. In addition, he is a successful business owner, entrepreneur and motivational speaker.

Born and raised in Santiago, Chile, Master Sies started his martial arts training at a very young age. At the age of eighteen, he earned the Chilean National Champion title, and at age twenty-one, he came to America in pursuit of a world championship title. He retired from professional kickboxing in 2005 after earning seven world championship titles.

Marco currently resides with his family in Potomac, Maryland, where he continues to teach and motivate students, individuals and companies.